Computer Vision for the Web

Unleash the power of Computer Vision algorithms in JavaScript to develop vision-enabled web content

Foat Akhmadeev

[PACKT] open source
PUBLISHING
community experience distilled

BIRMINGHAM - MUMBAI

Computer Vision for the Web

First published: October 2015

Production reference: 1091015

Published by Packt Publishing Ltd.
Livery Place
35 Livery Street
Birmingham B3 2PB, UK.

ISBN 978-1-78588-617-1

www.packtpub.com

Credits

Author
Foat Akhmadeev

Reviewer
Noritsuna Imamura

Acquisition Editor
Tushar Gupta

Content Development Editor
Amey Varangaonkar

Technical Editor
Vivek Pala

Copy Editor
Pranjali Chury

Project Coordinator
Francina Pinto

Proofreader
Safis Editing

Indexer
Mariammal Chettiyar

Graphics
Disha Haria

Production Coordinator
Arvindkumar Gupta

Cover Work
Arvindkumar Gupta

About the Author

Foat Akhmadeev has 5 years of experience in software development and research. He completed his master's degree in the year 2014 from the Kazan Federal University, Russia. He has worked on different projects, including development of high-loaded websites written in Java and real-time object detection for mobile phones. He has an extensive background in the field of Computer Vision. He has also written a scientific paper on 3D reconstruction from a single image. For more information, you can visit his website at `http://foat.me`.

About the Reviewer

Noritsuna Imamura is a specialist in embedded Linux/Android-based Computer Vision, and is one of the main members of SIProp.org (http://siprop.org/). His main works are as follows:

- ITRI Smart Glass, which is similar to Google Glass. He worked on this using Android 4.3 and OpenCV 2.4 in June 2014 (https://www.itri.org.tw/chi/Content/techTransfer/tech_tran_cont.aspx?&SiteID=1&MmmID=620622510147005345&Keyword=&MSid=4858).

- The Treasure Hunting Robot, a brainwave controlling robot that he developed in February 2012 (http://www.siprop.org/en/2.0/index.php?product%2FTreasureHuntingRobot).

- OpenCV for Android NDK. This has been included since Android 4.0.1 (http://tools.oesf.biz/android-4.0.1_r1.0/search?q=SIProp).

- The Auto Chasing Turtle, a human face recognition robot with Kinect, which he developed in February 2011 (http://www.siprop.org/ja/2.0/index.php?product%2FAutoChasingTurtle).

- Feel Sketch—an AR Authoring Tool and AR Browser as an Android application, which he developed in December 2009 (http://code.google.com/p/feelsketch/).

He can be contacted via e-mail at noritsuna@siprop.org.

www.PacktPub.com

Support files, eBooks, discount offers, and more

For support files and downloads related to your book, please visit www.PacktPub.com.

Did you know that Packt offers eBook versions of every book published, with PDF and ePub files available? You can upgrade to the eBook version at www.PacktPub.com and as a print book customer, you are entitled to a discount on the eBook copy. Get in touch with us at service@packtpub.com for more details.

At www.PacktPub.com, you can also read a collection of free technical articles, sign up for a range of free newsletters and receive exclusive discounts and offers on Packt books and eBooks.

https://www2.packtpub.com/books/subscription/packtlib

Do you need instant solutions to your IT questions? PacktLib is Packt's online digital book library. Here, you can search, access, and read Packt's entire library of books.

Why subscribe?

- Fully searchable across every book published by Packt
- Copy and paste, print, and bookmark content
- On demand and accessible via a web browser

Free access for Packt account holders

If you have an account with Packt at www.PacktPub.com, you can use this to access PacktLib today and view 9 entirely free books. Simply use your login credentials for immediate access.

Table of Contents

Preface

Computer Vision is one of the popular areas in computer science that have gained widespread importance lately. Besides, the power of personal computers has grown, thus opening the gate for developers to use Computer Vision algorithms directly on end user machines using client-side scripting. Nowadays, the most popular programming language for the web is JavaScript. It allows us to develop complex algorithms and run them directly in a web browser; this solves several major problems—the user needs nothing but a browser to run a web application, and as a developer, you get a lower load on your server. In this book, we will provide a comprehensive overview of the most popular JavaScript libraries and discuss the techniques they provide to help you in your initial steps in exciting fields, such as image processing and Computer Vision. This book covers Computer Vision methods by providing an intuitive overview of each algorithm and showing clear examples of the usage of libraries.

What this book covers

Chapter 1, Math Never Was So Simple! covers most of the necessary math operations that you need for using Computer Vision libraries and developing your own application.

Chapter 2, Turning Your Browser into Photoshop, introduces the most popular image processing techniques that are commonly used in the Computer Vision area.

Chapter 3, Easy Object Detection for Everyone, provides a detailed overview of object detection in photos and videos, starting from the basic examples, such as detecting objects by color, to the more complex examples such as feature detection.

Chapter 4, Smile and Wave, Your Face Has Been Tracked! covers detection of the face and face particles. In addition to this, it gives you an example of head tracking.

Chapter 5, May JS Be with You! Control Your Browser with Motion, extends the topic of object detection to object tracking and provides exhaustive examples. It also demonstrates how to create a human interface using gestures or head motion.

Chapter 6, What's Next? summarizes all that we will do throughout this book. Moreover, it provides references to several libraries that are not presented here.

What you need for this book

This book provides an overview of various methods in the Computer Vision area using JavaScript. Knowledge of JavaScript at the beginner level is required. It is totally fine if you know nothing about Computer Vision. However, you will need some basic math knowledge to understand the concepts in the book. To start with, you just need a web browser and your favorite text editor. This book will guide you from the basics of Computer Vision to the most complex algorithms in the JavaScript world.

Who this book is for

You will find this book interesting if you want a much easier way to use the power of Computer Vision in web applications. It will also be beneficial for those who want to implement a human interface on their websites, for example, to create a game. Even if you do not want to add the Computer Vision functionality to your website, take a look at what we have here—websites with Computer Vision algorithms will probably be a trend in the future. Even now you can benefit from using client-side scripting for Computer Vision—you will not need to buy extra machines for your backend.

Conventions

In this book, you will find a number of styles of text that distinguish between different kinds of information. Here are some examples of these styles, and an explanation of their meaning.

Code words in text are shown as follows: "The installation of a JavaScript library is straightforward. You just need to add a script file to your `<head>` tag."

A block of code is set as follows:

```
var dataBuffer = new jsfeat.data_t(cols * rows, imageData.data.
buffer);
var mat = new jsfeat.matrix_t(cols, rows, jsfeat.U8C4_t, dataBuffer);
var gray = tracking.Image.grayscale(mat.data, cols, rows, true);
```

New terms and important words are shown in bold.

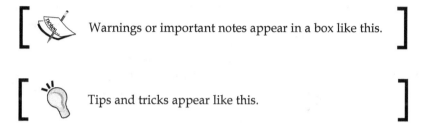

[Warnings or important notes appear in a box like this.]

[Tips and tricks appear like this.]

Reader feedback

Feedback from our readers is always welcome. Let us know what you think about this book—what you liked or may have disliked. Reader feedback is important for us to develop titles that you really get the most out of.

To send us general feedback, simply send an e-mail to feedback@packtpub.com, and mention the book title via the subject of your message. If there is a topic that you have expertise in and you are interested in either writing or contributing to a book, see our author guide on www.packtpub.com/authors.

Customer support

Now that you are the proud owner of a Packt book, we have a number of things to help you to get the most from your purchase.

Downloading the example code

You can download the example code files for all Packt books you have purchased from your account at http://www.packtpub.com. If you purchased this book elsewhere, you can visit http://www.packtpub.com/support and register to have the files e-mailed directly to you. Download link for the book: https://github.com/foat/computer-vision-for-the-web.

Downloading the color images of this book

We also provide you with a PDF file that has color images of the screenshots/diagrams used in this book. The color images will help you better understand the changes in the output. You can download this file from https://www.packtpub.com/sites/default/files/downloads/B05004_Computer_Vision_for_the_Web_ColorImage.pdf.

Errata

Although we have taken every care to ensure the accuracy of our content, mistakes do happen. If you find a mistake in one of our books—maybe a mistake in the text or the code—we would be grateful if you would report this to us. By doing so, you can save other readers from frustration and help us improve subsequent versions of this book. If you find any errata, please report them by visiting http://www.packtpub.com/submit-errata, selecting your book, clicking on the **errata submission form** link, and entering the details of your errata. Once your errata are verified, your submission will be accepted and the errata will be uploaded on our website, or added to any list of existing errata, under the Errata section of that title. Any existing errata can be viewed by selecting your title from http://www.packtpub.com/support.

Piracy

Piracy of copyright material on the Internet is an ongoing problem across all media. At Packt, we take the protection of our copyright and licenses very seriously. If you come across any illegal copies of our works, in any form, on the Internet, please provide us with the location address or website name immediately so that we can pursue a remedy.

Please contact us at copyright@packtpub.com with a link to the suspected pirated material.

We appreciate your help in protecting our authors, and our ability to bring you valuable content.

Questions

You can contact us at questions@packtpub.com if you are having a problem with any aspect of the book, and we will do our best to address it.

1
Math Never Was So Simple!

Computer Vision is all about math. When you need to create your own algorithm or implement something, you address a math topic. You should know how it works on the inside because without digging into the basics, it is hard to do anything. But you are not alone! Many smart people have created several useful libraries to simplify your job. One of those libraries is JSFeat (`http://inspirit.github.io/jsfeat/`), which has a realization of different math methods. Here, we will discuss fundamental elements of the library such as data structures, especially matrices, and simple math algorithms.

We will cover the following topics:

- Installation and core structure representation of JSFeat
- What is inside an image? All about matrices
- Useful functions and where to use them

Installation and core structure representation of JSFeat

JSFeat is a powerful tool to implement something new. To start using it, we need to initialize the project. It is relatively simple; if you have any experience with JavaScript, then it will not cause any trouble for you. The library itself contains various Computer Vision algorithms and it will be a good starting point for anyone who wants a flexible Computer Vision framework. First, you will learn how to install it and see a basic example of what you can do with the library.

Initializing the project

First of all, you need to download the JSFeat library and add it to your webpage. It is simple and it looks similar to this:

```html
<!doctype html>
<html>
<head>
    <meta charset="utf-8">
    <title>chapter1</title>
    <script src="js/jsfeat.js"></script>
</head>
<body></body></html>
```

As you can see, we just added a JavaScript library here without any additional actions. We do not need any particular software, since JavaScript is fast enough for many Computer Vision tasks.

The core data structure for the JSFeat library is a matrix. We will cover more topics about matrices in the next section, but to check whether everything works correctly, let's try to create an example.

Add the following code to a `<script/>` tag:

```javascript
var matrix = new jsfeat.matrix_t(3, 3, jsfeat.U8_t | jsfeat.C1_t);
matrix.data[1] = 1;
matrix.data[5] = 2;
matrix.data[7] = 1;
for (var i = 0; i < matrix.rows; ++i) {
  var start = i * matrix.cols;
  console.log(matrix.data.subarray(start, start + matrix.cols));
}
```

You will see the following in your console:

```
[0, 1, 0]
[0, 0, 2]
[0, 1, 0]
```

In the preceding code, we create a new matrix with the dimensions of 3 x 3 and an unsigned byte type with one channel. Next, we set a few elements into it and log the content of the matrix into the console row by row. The matrix data is presented as a one-dimensional array. Remember this, we will clarify it in the next section.

Finally, you did it! You have successfully added the JSFeat Computer Vision library to your first project. Now, we will discuss what a matrix actually is.

Understanding a digital image

It is likely that you already know that an image consists of pixels, which is a big step in understanding image processing. You already saw in the previous topics that a matrix is just a one-dimensional array. However, it represents two-dimensional array and its elements are presented in a row-major order layout. It is more efficient in terms of speed and memory to create a matrix in such a way. Our images are two dimensional too! Each pixel reflects the value of an array element. Consequently, it is obvious that a matrix is the best structure for image representation. Here, we will see how to work with a matrix and how to apply matrix conversion operations on an image.

Loading an image into a matrix

The JSFeat library uses its own data structure for matrices. First, we load an image using regular HTML and JavaScript operations. We then place a canvas on our webpage:

```
<canvas id="initCanvas"></canvas>
```

Then we need to place an image here. We do this with just a few lines of code:

```
var canvas = document.getElementById('initCanvas'),
    context = canvas.getContext('2d'),
    image = new Image();
image.src = 'path/to/image.jpg';

image.onload = function () {
    var cols = image.width;
    var rows = image.height;
    canvas.width = cols;
    canvas.height = rows;
    context.drawImage(image, 0, 0, image.width, image.height);
};
```

This is just a common way of displaying an image on a canvas. We define the image source path, and when the image is loaded, we set the canvas dimensions to those of an image and draw the image itself. Let's move on. Loading a canvas' content into a matrix is a bit tricky. Why is that? We need to use a `jsfeat.data_t` method, which is a data structure that holds a binary representation of an array. Anyway, since it is just a wrapper for the JavaScript ArrayBuffer, it should not be a problem:

```
var imageData = context.getImageData(0, 0, cols, rows);
var dataBuffer = new jsfeat.data_t(cols * rows, imageData.data.
buffer);
var mat = new jsfeat.matrix_t(cols, rows, jsfeat.U8_t | jsfeat.C4_t,
dataBuffer);
```

Here, we create a matrix as we did earlier, but in addition to that we add a new parameter, matrix buffer, which holds all the necessary data.

Probably, you already noticed that the third parameter for the matrix construction looks strange. It sets the type of matrix. Matrices have two properties:

- The first part represents the type of data in the matrix. In our example, it is `U8_t`; it states that we use unsigned byte array. Usually, an image uses 0-255 range for a color representation, that is why we need bytes here.

- Remember that an image consists of 3 main channels (red, green, and blue) and an alpha channel. The second part of the parameter shows the number of channels we use for the matrix. If there is only one channel, then it is a grayscale image.

How do we convert a colored image into a grayscale image? For the answer, we must move to the next section.

Basic matrix operations

Working with matrices is not easy. Who are we to fear the difficulties? With the help of this section, you will learn how to combine different matrices to produce interesting results.

Basic operations are really useful when you need to implement something new. Usually, Computer Vision uses grayscale images to work with them, since most Computer Vision algorithms do not need color information to track the object. As you may already know, Computer Vision mostly relies on the shape and intensity information to produce the results. In the following code, we will see how to convert a color matrix into a grayscale (one channel) matrix:

```
var gray = new jsfeat.matrix_t(mat.cols, mat.rows, jsfeat.U8_t |
jsfeat.C1_t);
jsfeat.imgproc.grayscale(mat.data, mat.cols, mat.rows, gray);
```

Just a few lines of code! First, we create an object, which will hold our grayscale image. Next, we apply the `JSFeat` function to that image. You may also define matrix boundaries for conversion, if you want. Here is the result of the conversion:

For this type of operation, you do not actually need to load a color image into the matrix; instead of `mat.data`, you can use `imageData.data` from the context—it's up to you.

To see how to display a matrix, refer to the *Matrix displaying* section.

One of the useful operations in Computer Vision is a matrix transpose, which basically just rotates a matrix by 90 degrees counter-clockwise. You need to keep in mind that the rows and columns of the original matrix are reflected during this operation:

```
var transposed = new jsfeat.matrix_t(mat.rows, mat.cols, mat.type |
mat.channel);
jsfeat.matmath.transpose(transposed, mat);
```

Downloading the example code

You can download the example code files for all Packt books you have purchased from your account at `http://www.packtpub.com`. If you purchased this book elsewhere, you can visit `http://www.packtpub.com/support` and register to have the files e-mailed directly to you. Download link for the book: `https://github.com/foat/computer-vision-for-the-web`.

Again, we need to predefine the resulting matrix, and only then we can apply the transpose operation:

Another operation that can be helpful is a matrix multiplication. Since it is hard to see the result on an image, we will fill matrices manually. The following code works by the formula $C = A * B$, the number of rows of the first matrix must be equal to the number of columns of the second matrix, e.g. MxN and NxK, those are dimensions for the first and the second matrices accordingly:

```
var A = new jsfeat.matrix_t(2, 3, jsfeat.S32_t | jsfeat.C1_t);
var B = new jsfeat.matrix_t(3, 2, jsfeat.S32_t | jsfeat.C1_t);
var C = new jsfeat.matrix_t(3, 3, jsfeat.S32_t | jsfeat.C1_t);
for (var i = 0; i < A.data.length; ++i) {
    A.data[i] = i + 1;
    B.data[i] = B.data.length / 2 - i;
}
jsfeat.matmath.multiply(C, A, B);
```

Here, the $M = K = 3$ and $N = 2$. Keep in mind that during the matrix creation, we place columns as a first parameter, and only as the second do we place rows. We populate matrices with dummy values and call the multiply function. After displaying the result in the console, you will see this:

```
[1, 2] [3,  2,  1] [ 3,  0, -3]
[3, 4] [0, -1, -2] [-3,  9,  2]
[5, 6]             [ 2, -5, 15]
```

Here the first column is matrix A, the second – matrix B and the third column is the result matrix of C.

JSFeat also provides such functions for matrix multiplication as `multiply_ABt`, `multiply_AAt`, and so on, where *t* means transposed. Use these functions when you do not want to write additional lines of code for the transpose method. In addition to this, there are matrix operations for 3 x 3 matrices, which are faster and optimized for this dimension. Besides, they are useful when, for example, you need to work with coordinates.

In the two-dimensional world, we use only x and y for coordinates. However, for more complex algorithms, when we need to define a point of intersection between two parallel lines, we need to add z (third) coordinate to a point, this system of coordinates is called homogeneous coordinates. They are especially helpful when you need to project a three-dimensional object onto a two-dimensional space.

Going deeper

Consider find features on an image, these features are usually used for object detection. There are many algorithms for this but you need a robust approach, which has to work with different object sizes. Moreover, you may need to reduce the redundancy of an image or search something the size of which you are unsure of. In that case, you need a set of images. The solution to this is a pyramid of an image. An **image pyramid** is a collection of several images, which are downsampled from the original.

The code for creating an image pyramid will look like this:

```
var levels = 4, start_width = mat.cols, start_height = mat.rows,
    data_type = jsfeat.U8_t | jsfeat.C1_t;
var pyramid = new jsfeat.pyramid_t(levels);
pyramid.allocate(start_width, start_height, data_type);
pyramid.build(mat);
```

First, we define the number of levels for the pyramid; here, we set it to 4. In JSFeat, the first level is skipped by default, since it is the original image. Next, we define the starting dimensions and output types. Then, we allocate space for the pyramid levels and build the pyramid itself. A pyramid is generally downsampled by a factor of 2:

JSFeat pyramid is just an array of matrices, it shows different pyramid layers starting from the original image and ending with the smallest image in the pyramid.

Matrix displaying

What we did not discuss in the previous section is how to display output matrices. It is done in different ways for grayscale and colored images. Here is the code for displaying matrices for a colored image:

```
var data = new Uint8ClampedArray(matColour.data);
var imageData = new ImageData(data, matColour.cols, matColour.rows);
context.putImageData(imageData, 0, 0);
```

We just need to cast the matrix data to the appropriate format and put the resulting `ImageData` function into the context. It is harder to do so for a grayscale image:

```
var imageData = new ImageData(mat.cols, mat.rows);
var data = new Uint32Array(imageData.data.buffer);
var alpha = (0xff << 24);
var i = mat.cols * mat.rows, pix = 0;
while (--i >= 0) {
    pix = mat.data[i];
    data[i] = alpha | (pix << 16) | (pix << 8) | pix;
}
```

This is a binary data representation. We populate the `ImageData` function with the alpha channel, which is constant for all pixels as well as for red, green, and blue channels. For a gray image, they have the same value, which is set as the `pix` variable. Finally, we need to put the `ImageData` function into the context as we did in the previous example.

Useful functions and where to use them

There are many functions that are needed in Computer Vision. Some of them are simple, such as sorting, while others are more complex. Here, we will discuss how to use them with the JSFeat library and see several Computer Vision applications.

Sorting using JSFeat

Sort algorithms are always helpful in any application. JSFeat provides an excellent way to sort a matrix. In addition to just sorting an array, it can even sort just part of the data. Let's see how we can do that:

1. First, we need to define a compare function, which is as follows:

```
var compareFunc = function (a, b) {
    return a < b;
};
```

2. Next, we do the sorting:

```
var length = mat.data.length;
jsfeat.math.qsort(mat.data, length / 3 * 2, length - 1,
compareFunc);
```

The first parameter defines an array for sorting, the second and third are the starting index and the ending index, respectively. The final parameter defines the comparison function. You will see the following image:

As we can see, the lower portion part of the image was sorted, looks good!

You will probably need a `median` function, which returns the number that separates the higher part of the data from the lower part. To understand this better, we need to see some examples:

```
var arr1 = [2, 3, 1, 8, 5];
var arr2 = [4, 6, 2, 9, -1, 6];
var median1 = jsfeat.math.median(arr1, 0, arr1.length - 1);
var median2 = jsfeat.math.median(arr2, 0, arr2.length - 1);
```

For the first array, the result is 3. It is simple. For the sorted array, number 3 just separates 1, 2 from 5, 8. What we do see for the second array, is the result of 4. Actually, different median algorithms may return different results; for the presented algorithm, JSFeat picks one of the array elements to return the result. In contrast, many approaches will return 5 in that case, since 5 represents the mean of two middle values (4, 6). Taking that into account, be careful and see how the algorithm is implemented.

Linear algebra

Who wants to solve a system of linear equations? No one? Don't worry, it can be done very easily.

First, let's define a simple linear system. To start with, we define the linear system as $Ax = B$, where we know A and B matrices and need to find x:

```
var bufA = [9, 6, -3, 2, -2, 4, -2, 1, -2],
    bufB = [6, -4, 0];

var A = new jsfeat.matrix_t(3, 3, jsfeat.F32_t | jsfeat.C1_t, new
jsfeat.data_t(bufA.length, bufA));
var B = new jsfeat.matrix_t(3, 1, jsfeat.F32_t | jsfeat.C1_t, new
jsfeat.data_t(bufB.length, bufB));

jsfeat.linalg.lu_solve(A, B);
```

JSFeat places the result into the B matrix, so be careful if you want to use B somewhere else or you will loose your data. The result will look like this:

```
[2.000..., -4.000..., -4.000..]
```

Since the algorithm works with floats, we cannot get the exact values but after applying a round operation, everything will look fine:

[2, -4, -4]

In addition to this, you can use the svd_solve function. In that case, you will need to define an X matrix as well:

```
jsfeat.linalg.svd_solve(A, X, B);
```

A perspective example

Let us show you a more catchy illustration. Suppose you have an image that is distorted by perspective or you want to rectify an object plane, for example, a building wall. Here's an example:

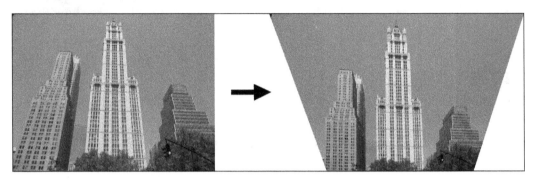

Looks good, doesn't it? How do we do that? Let's look at the code:

```
var imgRectified = new jsfeat.matrix_t(mat.cols, mat.rows, jsfeat.U8_t
| jsfeat.C1_t);
var transform = new jsfeat.matrix_t(3, 3, jsfeat.F32_t | jsfeat.C1_t);

jsfeat.math.perspective_4point_transform(transform,
        0, 0, 0, 0, // first pair x1_src, y1_src, x1_dst, y1_dst
        640, 0, 640, 0, // x2_src, y2_src, x2_dst, y2_dst and so on.
        640, 480, 640, 480,
        0, 480, 180, 480);
jsfeat.matmath.invert_3x3(transform, transform);
jsfeat.imgproc.warp_perspective(mat, imgRectified, transform, 255);
```

Primarily, as we did earlier, we define a result matrix object. Next, we assign a matrix for image perspective transformation. We calculate it based on four pairs of corresponding points. For example, the last, that is the fourth point of the original image, which is [0, 480], should be projected to the point of [180, 480] on the rectified image. Here, the first coordinate refers to X and the second to Y. Then, we invert the transform matrix to be able to apply it to the original image—mat variable. We pick the background color as white (255 for an unsigned byte). As a result, we get a nice image without any perspective distortion.

Summary

In this chapter, we saw many useful Computer Vision applications. Every time you want to implement something new, you need to start from the beginning. Fortunately, there are many libraries that can help you with your investigation. Here, we mainly covered the JSFeat library, since it provides basic methods for Computer Vision applications. We discussed how and when to apply the core of this library. Nevertheless, this is just a starting point, and if you want to see more exciting math topics and dig into the Computer Vision logic, we strongly encourage you to go through the next chapters of this book. See you there!

2
Turn Your Browser into Photoshop

It is likely that you have used Photoshop or at least heard about it. With a few clicks, you can easily modify an image, enhance it, or do some sort of preprocessing. Actually, it is not that hard to do using JavaScript. For most of the functions, you need only a couple lines of code. This chapter is mostly about filters and image segmentation. Here, we will discuss many popular techniques and their applications. Moreover, we will introduce a new JavaScript library—tracking.js (`http://trackingjs.com`). It is mostly used for object tracking applications, but there are many utilties, which are relevant to the topic. It is interesting to know how to use both JSFeat, which we introduced in the first chapter, and tracking.js libraries together. We will see how to do this. Besides, we will compare their advantages in terms of image filtering. We will start from the installation of the new library and then follow the filter examples from the easiest to the most exciting ones.

We will cover the following topics in this chapter:

- Introducing the tracking.js library
- What is filtering and how to use it
- Basic edge detection
- Advanced image processing

Introducing the tracking.js library

Let me give you a quick review of the tracking.js library. It is a great library that helps you with object detection, tracking, and image filtering. You can download it from `http://trackingjs.com`. In this section, we will focus on the the installation of the library and how both JSFeat and tracking.js libraries can be used together.

Installation and image loading

Actually, the installation of a JavaScript library is straightforward. You just need to add a script file to your `<head>` tag:

```
<script src="js/tracking.js"></script>
```

The image loading is done using the context, just like we did in the previous chapter:

```
var imageData = context.getImageData(0, 0, cols, rows);
```

In contrast to the JSFeat library, tracking.js works with arrays and it does not create a new object for images (as you remember, it is the `matrix_t` function for JSFeat). In that case, how do we apply a simple operation? Here is an example of how to convert a colored image to grayscale:

```
var gray = tracking.Image.grayscale(imageData.data, cols, rows, true);
```

The last parameter indicates whether you need to return the array in the RGBA format (`true`) or just in one channel grayscale (`false`). In that case, we receive a `Uint8ClampedArray`, which we can easily convert to the `ImageData` constructor and put it to the canvas context:

```
context.putImageData(new ImageData(gray, cols, rows), 0, 0);
```

Simple, isn't it? The only thing we should mention is that for most operations, tracking.js returns `Float32Array`. Generally, you can cast it to the unsigned byte array without losing any information.

Conversion between JSFeat and tracking.js image formats

In some cases JSFeat and tracking.js libraries complement each other. To benefit from using them together, you will probably need to convert a JSFeat matrix to an array and vice versa. The critical difference is that, even for a grayscale data, tracking.js sometimes uses four array elements: R, G, B, A.

To use a matrix as an array, we just need to get `mat.data` from a matrix. In the following code, we load matrix from the `ImageData` constructor and pass `mat.data` to the tracking.js grayscale function:

```
var dataBuffer = new jsfeat.data_t(cols * rows, imageData.data.
buffer);
var mat = new jsfeat.matrix_t(cols, rows, jsfeat.U8C4_t, dataBuffer);
var gray = tracking.Image.grayscale(mat.data, cols, rows, true);
```

Since the `mat` variable consists of four channels, we do not need to convert it to a different format. But what if we want to use the gray variable as a matrix?

```
var buf = new Array(gray.length / 4);
for (var i = 0, j = 0; i < gray.length; i += 4, ++j) {
    buf[j] = gray[i];
}
var matGray = new jsfeat.matrix_t(cols, rows, jsfeat.U8C1_t,
        new jsfeat.data_t(cols * rows, buf));
```

In that case, we skip G, B, A elements and add only R elements to the buffer. With that buffer, we then populate the one channel matrix.

As you can see, the conversion process is simple, just keep in mind that tracking.js usually uses 4-channel data.

What is filtering and how to use it?

Image filtering is always a powerful tool to use in your Computer Vision applications. It allows you to apply many exciting effects on your photos, such as image correction, noise reduction, embossing, and many more. Image filtering is actually a huge subpart of an image processing area. In this section, we will discuss the concepts of image filtering and talk about a basic operation—convolution, which is widely used in all Computer Vision applications. Furthermore, we will see how different effects, such as blurring, are achieved.

Image convolution

The core of most filtering operations is image convolution. With its understanding you will have the power to make your own image filters.

The image convolution idea is that you want to apply to each pixel of the original image a transformation which is based on neighboring pixels. For this, you have a kernel—a simple 2D matrix, this is our transformation matrix. For each pixel of the original image, we take the sum of products, each product is just a new value of a resulting image. To compute it, each element of the kernel should be multiplied with the corresponding image pixel, where the center of the kernel must be multiplied with the current pixel of an image. The whole process is called convolution.

To see a practical example of convolution, we should move to one of the most popular filters, it uses the **Gaussian kernel**. The filter itself is called a Gaussian filter (or Gaussian blur), and it is used for image smoothing, noise removing, and for edge detection. Most of the edge detection algorithms are sensitive to noise, using the Gaussian filter before the edge detection helps to remove unnecessary noise.

In the following figure, we present an example of convolution using the
Gaussian kernel:

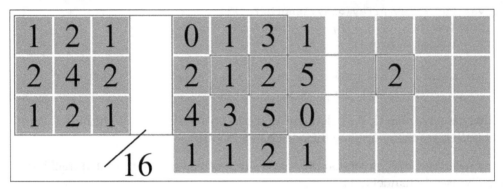

From left to right: the Gaussian kernel, original matrix, and result matrix.

To compute a value in the (2, 2) position of the result matrix, we do the convolution:

(1*0 + 2*1 + 1*3 + 2*2 + 4*1 + 2*2 + 1*4 + 2*3 + 1*5) / 16 = 2

See how the neighbors of the original matrix affect the result? Simply, a kernel matrix
represents weights for the transformation process.

The 2D convolution requires four loops to compute so, in that case, it is better not to
use big kernels; otherwise, our filtering process will be too slow. Usually, in image
processing, the kernels from *3x3* to *7x7* are used and, as we already mentioned, the
kernel should have a center and the dimensions should be odd. There are methods to
improve the performance of the convolution operation, and we will analyze one of
them in the next section.

The Gaussian filter and separate convolution

Normally, we do not want to use heavy processing methods, such as applying a 2D
kernel on an image. To speed up the computation, we can use a different approach.
For most of the Computer Vision applications, we need only some sort of blurring
and edge detection methods. In that case, the 2D kernels which are used there may
be presented as two separate 1D kernels. This type of operation states that you can
get the same result by applying two separate filters for rows and columns. The
process is called separate convolution. Here is an example of the Gaussian kernel:

```
[0.25]                        [0.0625,  0.125,   0.0625]
[0.5 ] X [0.25, 0.5, 0.25] =  [0.125,   0.0625,  0.125 ]
[0.25]                        [0.0625,  0.125,   0.25  ]
```

The 2D matrix is separable if it can be presented as the outer product of two vectors.

Enough of the theory! We did not even see the Gaussian filter in work. Moreover, it is a good point to combine both JSFeat and tracking.js libraries.

To get a Gaussian kernel, we will use JSFeat:

```
var kernelSize = 3, sigma = 0, kernelArray = [], dataType = jsfeat.
F32_t;
jsfeat.math.get_gaussian_kernel(kernelSize, sigma, kernelArray,
dataType);
```

You can get different sizes of a Gaussian kernel. The larger the size, the more blurry the image will be. Previously, we saw kernels only for the size of 3 elements. Next, sigma specifies how wide your blur will be. If you set it to 0, then the function calculates the optimal value for the given kernel size itself. The result is written to the kernelArray variable and, of course, the data type is float, since we are working with floating point operations. After executing the function, kernelArray will contain the following:

```
[0.25, 0.5, 0.25]
```

To get a full 2D kernel, we can use the multiply function, which we saw in the previous chapter:

```
var gaussianKernel = new jsfeat.data_t(kernelArray.length,
kernelArray);
var A = new jsfeat.matrix_t(1, kernelSize, jsfeat.F32C1_t,
gaussianKernel),
        B = new jsfeat.matrix_t(kernelSize, 1, jsfeat.F32C1_t,
gaussianKernel),
        C = new jsfeat.matrix_t(kernelSize, kernelSize, jsfeat.
F32C1_t);
jsfeat.matmath.multiply(C, A, B);
```

You can print C to see that it represents the Gaussian kernel.

To use 1D kernels, we need to apply filters one by one to the original image. Unfortunately, JSFeat library does not provide you with such functionality. But tracking.js does! We will do this as follows:

```
var buf = tracking.Image.horizontalConvolve(gray, cols, rows,
kernelArray, true);
buf = tracking.Image.verticalConvolve(buf, cols, rows, kernelArray,
true);
```

Remember that you need to set the last parameter to `true` if you want to return an RGBA array. Using the preceding code, we receive a blurred image, but what if we apply each filter separately? To see a clearer result, we need to choose a larger kernel size:

From left to right, we see a gray image and then we see a horizontal filter applied to it followed by a vertical filter for the the same gray image. Finally, if we apply both filters to the original image, as we did in the code, we will receive a blurred image like the last one. Eventually, the separate convolution works! It is really great to use that when you can present a 2D kernel as two 1D kernels.

It is worth mentioning that you can apply a Gaussian filter without using separate filters. For JSFeat library, see the following code:

```
jsfeat.imgproc.gaussian_blur(matGray, matBlurred, kernelSize);
```

For the tracking.js, see the following code:

```
var blurred = tracking.Image.blur(gray, cols, rows, kernelSize);
```

For the last one, the result returns `Float32Array`. So if you want to display it properly, you need to convert it to the `Uint8ClampedArray` type. In addition, this is the first function you see which returns RGBA values, you cannot return only one channel array here.

Here are the examples with different kernel sizes:

As you can see, the bigger the kernel size we take, the less the information we receive from an image and the blurrier it becomes.

The Gaussian filter is very useful when you need to reduce the image noise and reduce its details. Besides, it is commonly used to reduce the size of an image to get a better image approximation for a small size.

The box blur

There is a different blur method that needs to be discussed. Sometimes, you just need a rough approximation for the Gaussian Blur operation, a filter which is faster than Gaussian. Furthermore, you can sacrifice some blur quality. In that case, you can use the box blur filter.

This is just a regular mean operation. It has a simple kernel for a diameter of 3 elements:

```
[1/9, 1/9, 1/9]
[1/9, 1/9, 1/9]
[1/9, 1/9, 1/9]
```

So, for a diameter = d it will be like the following:

```
[1/n, 1/n, ..., 1/n]
[1/n, 1/n, ..., 1/n]
[..., ..., ..., ...]
[1/n, 1/n ..., 1/n]
```

Where, $n = d * d$ is the number of elements in a kernel.

It is simpler than Gaussian blur, but produces worse results. It is usually used as an approximation of a Gaussian blur. With the JSFeat library, it can be applied as follows:

```
jsfeat.imgproc.box_blur_gray(matGray, blurred, kernelRadius);
```

Here, we use a `kernelRadius` parameter instead of a diameter (matrix size). The same result can be achieved if you use the following:

```
[1/3, 1/3, 1/3]
```

Separate filter vector with tracking.js library. Actually, a close result to the Gaussian filter can be achieved if you apply box blur three times with a three times smaller kernel. For example, if the Gaussian kernel size is equal to 33 values, then the kernel size for the box blur should be 11 (or with radius = 5):

The first image has the Gaussian filter applied, the next has the box blur, which was applied thrice, and the last has the box blur with the same kernel size as the Gaussian kernel. Can you tell the difference between the first two images? It is really impossible to point it out. In addition, we see that the box blur for the last image removed more details and it produced an even worse result. Use the box blur filter only when you need to speed up the computation. But why is it so fast? There is magic in computing an integral image.

The integral image

Integrals are really useful when you need to compute image parameters quickly. For example, you can compute a filtered image for the box blur filter using the same amount of processing time for any kernel size. Isn't this amazing? Furthermore, it is also used for object detection.

Computing the integral image is just a simple algorithm that generates sums of values in rectangular subsets of a matrix. For the JSFeat library, it can be computed like this:

```
var matCopy1 = new jsfeat.matrix_t(matGray.cols + 1, matGray.rows + 1,
jsfeat.F32C1_t);
var matCopy2 = new jsfeat.matrix_t(matGray.cols + 1, matGray.rows + 1,
jsfeat.F32C1_t);
var matCopy3 = new jsfeat.matrix_t(matGray.cols + 1, matGray.rows + 1,
jsfeat.F32C1_t);

jsfeat.imgproc.compute_integral_image(matGray, matCopy1.data,
matCopy2.data, matCopy3.data);
```

The first matrix will contain the integral image or regular sums of image subsets, the next matrix will contain squares of those sums, and the last will contain the tilted integral image. The dimensions of all input matrices should be 1 pixel larger than the original. To display the result, we need to normalize it, for example, the bottom-right element will contain the sum of all pixel values in a matrix. We cannot display the result matrix because the largest possible pixel value of an image is 255. We need to divide each pixel by the maximum value in a matrix and multiply it by 255. Here is the result:

We got what we expected—the maximum value is situated in the bottom-right corner for the first two matrices and the tilted result is presented in the last.

You can apply a box blur using integrals by yourself! Here is a simple explanation of how to do this:

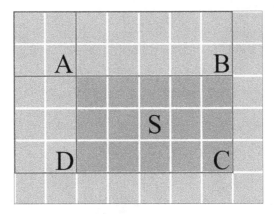

We need to compute the sum in the ABCD rectangle. From the integral image, we know which sums are stored in A, B, C, and D positions. The sum of the rectangle can be computed using the following formula:

$S = value\ in\ C - value\ in\ B - value\ in\ D + value\ in\ A$

This can be applied to any size of the box blur filter, and this is why it is that fast. First, we need to compute an integral image, which is done in one loop over all pixel values and then we just calculate S for each pixel.

Basic edge detection

For most Computer Vision applications, you process an image but you do not actually need to get all the information from it. For example, sometimes you just need to get the shape information to find an appropriate object. There is a huge topic in the field of image processing called **edge detection**. Methods related to that topic, search for points where pixel brightness changes dramatically. The extracted information aims to capture changes in the properties of an image. To understand the concept better and to see how the basic edge information can be extracted from an image, we will discuss different edge filters (or operators) starting with the Sobel filter.

The Sobel filter

The Sobel operator or Sobel filter is common and widely used. It helps to detect edges and transitions in images. The Sobel operator uses two kernels during the processing — one for horizontal changes in brightness and another for vertical changes. Its kernel values are focused not on the current pixel, but on it neighboring pixels.

Typical Sobel kernels look like this:

```
[-1,  0,  1]    [1]                  [-1,  -2,  -1]    [-1]
[-2,  0,  2] = [2] X [-1,  0,  1]    [ 0,   0,   0] = [ 0] X [1, 2, 1]
[-1,  0,  1]    [1]                  [ 1,   2,   1]    [ 1]
```

As you see, the kernels can be decomposed of two separate filters, which is good in terms of processing time. You can run this filter in different ways in the libraries. Since tracking.js provides more functionality with separable filters, let's see some of its examples:

```
var sobelSignVector = [-1, 0, 1];
var sobelScaleVector = [1, 2, 1];
var horizontal = tracking.Image.separableConvolve(gray, cols, rows,
sobelScaleVector, sobelSignVector, true);
var vertical = tracking.Image.separableConvolve(gray, cols, rows,
sobelSignVector, sobelScaleVector, true);
```

This is another way of applying separable filters in tracking.js library. We use the `separableConvolve` function, whereas for the fourth and fifth parameters, it uses Sobel vectors.

The results are usually called derivatives, since they measure the change in values. We can compute these derivatives in JSFeat as follows:

```
jsfeat.imgproc.sobel_derivatives(matGray, imgGxGy);
```

Where `imgGxGy` returns a 2-channel matrix, the first channel represents horizontal derivatives and the second represents vertical derivatives.

To get the result of a Sobel filter, we need to combine those two results; this is done using the following equation:

```
var value = Math.sqrt(h * h + v * v);
```

Here, the value variable is the value of each pixel and it is computed using pixel values from horizontal and vertical derivatives.

To run the Sobel operator on an image directly you may prefer to use the following tracking.js function:

```
var sobelImg = tracking.Image.sobel(gray, cols, rows);
```

You need to remember that it returns an RGBA array and you need to normalize it, since it contains values larger than 255.

The final result will look like this:

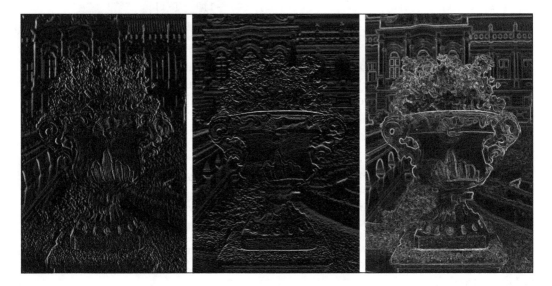

From left to right, we see the horizontal derivative, followed by the vertical derivative, and finally, the result after applying the Sobel filter. As you can see, the edges of the image have a good visualization. To get edges, not just changes in image pixels, we need to go a bit deeper. But let's discuss several other useful operators that you may want to use in edge detection.

Other operators

You need to keep in mind that in Computer Vision, there is usually no perfect way for doing things. There are several operators that need to be mentioned; in some cases, they can produce better results than the Sobel filter. For example, the Prewitt operator:

```
[-1, 0, 1]   [1]                        [-1, -1, -1]   [-1]
[-1, 0, 1] = [1] X [-1, 0, 1]           [ 0,  0,  0] = [ 0] X [1, 1, 1]
[-1, 0, 1]   [1]                        [ 1,  1,  1]   [ 1]
```

Sometimes, it is a good point to start from, but it averages the result value too much, remember the box blur filter? Compare it with the Gaussian Blur, where the center of a kernel has more weight. If we want to do that, the Sobel filter is preferred. However, sometimes you need to save just a bit more information for the center. And if you need that, you can use the Scharr filter:

```
[ -3, 0,  3]   [ 3]                [-3, -10, -3]   [-1]
[-10, 0, 10] = [10] X [-1, 0, 1]   [ 0,  0,   0] = [ 0] X [3, 10, 3]
[ -3, 0,  3]   [ 3]                [ 3,  10,  3]   [ 1]
```

See, the centre has more weight now. Actually, it is difficult to see the difference between Prewitt, Sobel and Sharr operators, which is why we don't have visual examples here. It is better to perform some experiments and check which filter you need exactly.

Advanced image processing

We talked about filters a lot, but they usually require only some sort of a matrix kernel and that is it. If you think that there should be more cool stuff in image filtering, you are totally right! First, we will see how to apply edge detection and how it works. In the final part, we will review the histogram equalization algorithm, which you probably use a lot if you have Photoshop.

The Canny edge detector

Let's be curious; what if we threshold an image after the Sobel filter? Thresholding is done by iterating over all pixels of a grayscale image and checking whether the value exceeds the threshold value:

```
for (var i = 0; i < arr.length; i++)
    arr[i] = arr[i] > threshold ? 255 : 0;
```

This is what the threshold looks like. Just set the value to 255 if it is higher than the threshold and to 0 when it is not.

Here are several examples of different thresholds, each image having a higher threshold value than the previous:

See? The higher the threshold we set, the fewer the edges we get. This is the first step of the Canny edge detection algorithm.

When you need to process only the most important information from images (it is usually shape information), and you need to remove unnecessary data without losing the important structural properties of an image, it is really smart to use an edge detector. Nowadays, the Canny edge detector is used most commonly.

You can run the whole algorithm using the JSFeat library:

```
var canny = new jsfeat.matrix_t(cols, rows, jsfeat.U8C1_t);
jsfeat.imgproc.gaussian_blur(matGray, canny, kernelSize);
jsfeat.imgproc.canny(canny, canny, lowThresh, highThresh);
```

Before the start of a Canny algorithm we usually apply the Gaussian Blur to reduce the noise. The larger you choose the kernel size, the fewer edges and less noise you get. Lower and higher thresholds are usually chosen empirically.

Under the lower threshold, all pixels (weak pixels) are removed (or suppressed) by the algorithm, as we did while playing with the Sobel filter thresholding. Pixels with a value larger than the higher threshold are marked as strong pixels. At the last stage, in addition to weak pixels, the algorithm suppress all pixels that are not connected to those strong pixels. As a rule of thumb, the smaller your lower threshold is, the more noise you get; the larger your higher threshold is, the fewer the object edges you receive. This is shown in the following figure:

The algorithm detects object boundaries or edges. For the first image, we picked 50 and 300 as the lower and higher thresholds, respectively, and we did not use the Gaussian Blur. For the second image, we applied the Gaussian filter. As a result, many noise edges were removed. If we increase the lower threshold to 100, then we will get the result from the third image. In that case, much of the noise data from the ground is removed. After increasing the higher threshold, we get fewer object edges, which can be seen in the fourth image. You can play with parameters; just remember that when you increase any of the thresholds, you receive less information.

The Canny filter returns only 0 for background and 255 for edges. The thickness of the edges is 1 pixel, which is really important when you need to find an object. The Canny edge detector is included in many Computer Vision frameworks and its application is very wide. It is adaptive to various environment conditions and it is very robust.

Histogram equalization

Sometimes, you may want to improve the contrast of an image. It helps to see the details better when the important data is represented by close contrast values. The help comes from methods that operate with image histograms. An image histogram presents the number of pixels for each tonal value. Suppose you have an array, as follows:

```
var arr = [30, 100, 10, 30, 30, 100, 50, 255];
```

You may want to redistribute values in case they have a better spreading of their intensity values. Let's use the histogram equalization method which is provided by JSFeat:

```
var matGray = new jsfeat.matrix_t(arr.length, 1, jsfeat.U8C1_t,
        new jsfeat.data_t(arr.length, arr));
var equalized = new jsfeat.matrix_t(arr.length, 1, jsfeat.U8C1_t);
jsfeat.imgproc.equalize_histogram(matGray, equalized);
```

Histogram equalization is just a usual function. The first parameter indicates the input matrix, the second indicates the output equalized matrix. With our array, we receive as a result of equalization `equalized.data`:

```
[128, 223, 32, 128, 128, 223, 159, 255]
```

The histogram for the original (left) and equalized (right) arrays will look like this:

```
 10: 1         32: 1
 30: 3        128: 3
 50: 1        159: 1
100: 2        223: 2
255: 1        255: 1
```

The equalize histogram function maps old values to the new ones, performing a better spread over the whole range of values, 0-255. In the preceding example, most of the values were situated in the first part of the range, after the redistribution, the difference between values was increased. Visually, it helps to distinguish separate image objects.

Here is how it looks with an image:

Left – the original grayscale image, and right – the image after equalization.

As you can see, the contrast is much better now and the image itself looks more impressive. The grass and plants got much darker and the constructions are brighter. The histograms for the input and output images are as follows:

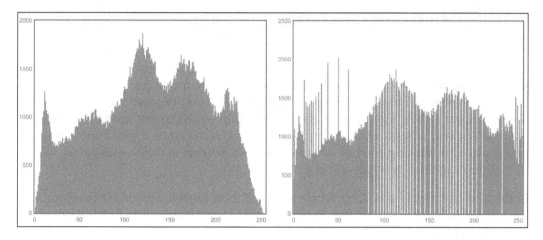

As a consequence of better spreading, histogram equalization makes the histogram a bit more flat, so the histogram values do not have such a clear center.

Histogram equalization can be used not only for a better image view, but also for extracting better image information. It is usually useful when an image background and foreground do not have high contrast. The biggest drawback that you should know is that this function may increase image noise. Anyway, histogram equalization is really useful, for example, in medical imaging and photo correction.

Summary

In this chapter, you first learned how to install tracking.js and how to use it with JSFeat. Now you know how to create your own image filters using the image convolution operation. Moreover, with separable convolutions, you can create much faster implementations of regular filters. When you need to reduce the noise, you will commonly use the Gaussian filter or the box blur filter when you need a faster algorithm. Edge detection? No problem, you can implement it and use it in your applications for both cases, when you need only the edges or the whole information about a change in image brightness. Last but not least, you now know how to improve the image contrast using histogram equalization. Look at how much we have covered in such a small chapter! There are many more topics on image processing and filtering, we just discussed a small portion of it. Eventually, we will be ready to use this knowledge in object detection.

In the next chapter, you will learn how to detect various objects using different tracking techniques, such as color detection and feature estimation. In addition, we will be able to create our own tracker. See you there!

3
Easy Object Detection for Everyone

In the last chapter, We discussed fundamental topics such as matrix operations and matrix convolutions. Moreover, we saw how to apply various image filters and how to use them in our applications. But those topics are mostly about image processing, not about Computer Vision! What do Computer Vision methods do by themselves? They provide the ability to understand an image by analyzing it in such a manner that the computer can provide the information about objects of an image scene. Libraries, which we discussed previously, provide various functionalities to find different objects in an image. In this chapter, we will mainly discuss methods that are included in the tracking. js (http://trackingjs.com) and JSFeat (http://inspirit.github.io/jsfeat/) libraries to get objects from an image. We will see how to find a colored object, and how to find an object using a template. Further, we will create our own object detector. These techniques can be implemented not only for an image, but for a video too! Finally, we will move on to the object tracking topic.

We will cover the following topics in this chapter:

- Color object detection
- Digging into the tracking.js API
- Image features
- Descriptors and object matching

Detecting color objects

In the previous chapters, we worked mainly with grayscale images. Of course, the shape and intensity parts of objects are important, but what about the color information? Why don't we use that too? For example, a red apple on a table can be easily detected with just the color information. Actually, that is why color object detection sometimes performs much better than other detector methods. In addition, it is much faster to implement these algorithms, and a computer usually consumes less resources for these types of operation.

The tracking.js library provides an outstanding functionality to create a color detection application. We will start from a basic color tracking example. It is relatively simple, but you need to keep in mind that it performs best only when a colored object can be easily separated from the background.

Using predefined colors with the tracking.js library

Color detection is one of the methods provided by tracking.js. To use it properly, we need to learn some background first.

We will start with the intuitive steps:

1. First, we find all connected regions with the specified color. This is the most computation consuming part of the algorithm. The smaller the color regions present on an image, the faster the algorithm works.

2. Next, we define bounding boxes or rectangles around each of those regions. Finally, we merge overlapping boxes to find the main object. Merging is done by just one pass. So, if an image has overlapping boxes that are produced after the first merge, then they will still overlap each other.

We will run the algorithm using three colors: yellow, magenta, and cyan. Here is an example of the color detection algorithm:

As you can see, it is really hard to get color objects from the first image. It is a bit easier to do so for the second, but it can be easily done only for the center of the flower, since it can be separated from the leaves and flower petals.

How can we do that with the tracking.js library? In this example, we will use the canvas, as we did in the previous chapters. It can be done for other tags too, which we will see a bit in the following.

First, we define a `ColorTracker` object and add prebuilt colors to it. For now, there are only three colors available: `magenta`, `cyan`, and `yellow`.

```
var canvas = document.getElementById('initCanvas');
var tracker = new tracking.ColorTracker(['magenta', 'cyan',
'yellow']);
```

The tracker variable is just a holder for various parameters, based on which we will track an object.

Then, we need to define a function which will be called after the `track` event. In the example, we just want to show all our bounding boxes over the canvas and we execute the `draw` function for each rectangle here. Since the algorithm returns a color for a box, it will be easier to see the difference between results:

```
tracker.on('track', function (event) {
    event.data.forEach(function (rect) {
        draw(rect.x, rect.y, rect.width, rect.height, rect.color);
    });
});
```

As we did in the first chapter, we create a `<div>` element for our canvas:

```
<div id="images" class="canvas-parent">
    <canvas id="initCanvas" class="canvas-img"></canvas>
</div>
```

There are many ways of printing a result, for now, we take an example of the draw function from the tracking.js examples section. It will create a `<div>` element for each bounding box and append it to the `<div>` tag around the canvas:

```
var canvasParent = document.querySelector('.canvas-parent');
function draw(x, y, w, h, color) {
    var rect = document.createElement('div');
    canvasParent.appendChild(rect);
    rect.classList.add('rect');
    rect.style.border = '8px solid ' + color;
    rect.style.width = w + 'px';
    rect.style.height = h + 'px';
    rect.style.left = (canvas.offsetLeft + x) + 'px';
    rect.style.top = (canvas.offsetTop + y) + 'px';
    rect.style.position = 'absolute';
}
```

Finally, we only need to start the tracker by calling the `track` function. The first parameter defines the element that contains graphical information about where we need to detect a color. The second parameter holds the `tracker` variable:

```
tracking.track('#initCanvas', tracker);
```

It was simple, wasn't it? We saw how the tracker works with not-so-easy examples. It can be applied for those cases, but it will not be smart to do that. Let's see examples where the color detection works really well.

Using your own colors

Only three colors?! Is that it? Of course not. If you want, you can register your own colors for object detection. It is not much harder than setting predefined colors. We first need to register a new color for the `ColorTracker` function. You create a mapping between a string and a function, where the function should return a Boolean condition based on three channels: R, G, and B. The `true` is returned when the color matches our condition and `false` if not. Here, we want to get all colors where the red channel prevails. Since we start from really dark pixels, we will call it the `darkRed` color:

```
tracking.ColorTracker.registerColor('darkRed', function (r, g, b) {
    return r > 100 && g < 90 && b < 90;
});
```

By doing that, we register the darkRed color for all color trackers which we create. Now, we need to define a new color tracker with the newly registered color:

```
var tracker = new tracking.ColorTracker(['darkRed']);
```

All other parts of the code are the same as they were in the previous example. The good thing is that the tracking.js library itself finds the color for a bounding box, we do not need to specify it. For example, we have picked a new image—two beautiful apples and the result looks something like the following screenshot:

Do you see how the apples stand out from the cloth? That is an example of an image where color tracker shows its best performance. Use the color detection when an object can be easily separated from the background and you will not be disappointed. Furthermore, the basic advantages are that color detection is fast in terms of computation, and it is very easy to implement.

Digging into the tracking.js API

We saw a color tracker and added our own color matcher. The tracking.js library provides an excellent functionality to add a new object detector. It has a clear API and good documentation to follow (`http://trackingjs.com/docs.html`). But first, we will see how to use a tracker with different HTML tags and dig a bit into the tracker API.

Using the <img> and <video> tags

The library uses a `<canvas>` tag to operate with images. If you run a tracker on a different tag, then the library will convert the information from it to the canvas automatically.

First of all, tracking can be applied to an `<img>` tag:

```
<img id="img" src="/path/to/your/image.jpg"/>
```

In that case, we can specify the image path not in a JavaScript code, but in the tag itself. To run a tracker, we just need to set the tag `id` as a first parameter:

```
tracking.track('#img', tracker);
```

Next comes the `<video>` tag. In our `<div>` element, which wraps the canvas, we need to add a `<video>` tag with the path to a video file:

```
<div id="images" class="canvas-parent">

    <video id="video" preload autoplay loop muted controls>
        <source src="/path/to/your/video">
    </video>
    <canvas id="initCanvas" class="canvas-img"></canvas>
</div>
```

The library will take each frame and process it separately. If we want to print the result on a canvas, we need to clear the canvas of the previous tracking results. We can do that using the `context.clearRect` function and add it to the postprocessing part of the tracker functionality:

```
var context = canvas.getContext('2d');
tracker.on('track', function (event) {
    context.clearRect(0, 0, canvas.width, canvas.height);
    event.data.forEach(function (rect) {
        draw(rect.x, rect.y, rect.width, rect.height, rect.color);
    });
});
```

We can draw new elements not only with the `<div>` tags, but also using the context itself. It is easier to use and the speed will be a bit faster. Here, in addition to just displaying a bounding box, we place a rectangle parameter around it:

```
function draw(x, y, w, h, color) {
    context.strokeStyle = color;
    context.strokeRect(x, y, w, h);
    context.fillStyle = "#fff";
    context.fillText('x: ' + x + 'px', x + w + 5, y + 11);
}
```

To run the tracker with a video file, we place the `id` parameters of a `<video>` tag, as we did previously with other content tags:

```
tracking.track('#video', tracker);
```

If you want to work with a camera instead of a video file, you need to remove the source from a `<video>` tag and add a new, third, parameter to the `track` call:

```
tracking.track('#video', tracker, { camera: true });
```

What if you have a long-running video? In that case, you probably need to have full control over your application, as you may want to stop and rerun the tracker. First, you need to get a reference to it:

```
var trackingTask = tracking.track(...);
```

You can stop or run a tracking task any time with those functions:

```
trackingTask.stop();
trackingTask.run();
```

If you are still not satisfied with your control over the tracking methods, there are various functions that can help you while you do the tracking:

- `setMinDimension`: This sets a bounding box of an object with minimum width and height; by default, it is 20 pixels. It helps to avoid noisy objects and focuses on objects that hold a larger space.

- `setMaxDimension`: This sets the maximum dimensions of a bounding box, it is infinity by default. In some cases, it helps to remove an image background which is of the same color as the object.

- `setMinGroupSize`: This sets the minimum number of pixels for a colored object to be classified as a rectangle; the default is 30. This also helps to reduce the noise significantly.

Building a custom tracker

It is time to build your own tracker! The tracking.js library provides an abstract interface for that, but you need to write the core of the tracker—its brains. We will create a tracker that will determine edge pixels using the knowledge that you gained from the previous chapter.

As a first step, we will create a constructor of our new CornerTracker variable. We will use the Sobel filter for our example, so we only need one threshold parameter for it, which we define here as a field of our object:

```
var CornerTracker = function (thres) {
    CornerTracker.base(this, 'constructor');
    this.thres = thres;
};
```

Our tracker must inherit from the basic tracker of the tracking.js library, which can be done using the following function:

```
tracking.inherits(CornerTracker, tracking.Tracker);
```

The most important part of our tracker is a track function. It contains the tracker logic. As parameters, it takes an array of pixels from an image and the dimensions of that image. On the inside, we run the Sobel filter, and if you remember, it returns a 4-channel array for a grayscale image, but we need only one. We check whether the value exceeds the threshold and if so, we add a new edge pixel there. After all, we need to emit the computed data using the emit function. It sends the output data through the track event. The output for our example is the coordinates of pixels that passed the condition:

```
CornerTracker.prototype.track = function (pixels, width, height) {
    var sobel = tracking.Image.sobel(pixels, width, height);
    var edges = [];
    var pos = 0;
    for (var i = 0; i < height; i++) {
        for (var j = 0; j < width; j++) {
            var w = i * width * 4 + j * 4;
            if (sobel[w] > this.thres)
                edges[pos++] = {x: j, y: i};
        }
    }
    this.emit('track', {
        data: edges
    });
};
```

To create a new tracker, we call the constructor with a threshold parameter and set the threshold to 400:

```
var tracker = new CornerTracker(400);
```

At the end of tracking process, we plot the result. The plot function simply puts the pixels on a canvas:

```
tracker.on('track', function (event) {
    event.data.forEach(function (point) {
        plot(point.x, point.y);
    });
});

var context = canvas.getContext('2d');
function plot(x, y) {
    context.fillStyle = '#FF0000';
    context.fillRect(x, y, 3, 3);
}
```

To start our tracker, we need to initiate the tracking function as we did previously:

```
tracking.track('#initCanvas', tracker);
```

Let's match the result from the previous chapter with our tracker:

From left to right: an image after the Sobel filter, Sobel filter thresholding and the result after our tracker.

As we see, the results match together, so we have done everything right. Good job!

The tracking.js API provides a very good abstraction level for creating your own object tracker. There are not many trackers there yet, but you can always extend the functionality. The main advantage of this abstraction is that you can focus on the implementation of algorithms without wasting your time thinking about how to apply your algorithm to an image.

Image features

Color object detection and detection of changes in intensity of an image, is a simple Computer Vision method. It is a fundamental thing which every Computer Vision enthusiast should know. To get a better picture of Computer Vision capabilities, we will see how to find an object on a scene using a template. This topic includes several parts: feature extraction and descriptor matching. In this part, we will discuss feature detection and its application in Computer Vision.

Detecting key points

What information do we get when we see an object on an image? An object usually consists of some regular parts or unique points, which represent the particular object. Of course, we can compare each pixel of an image, but it is not a good idea in terms of computational speed. We can probably take unique points randomly, thus reducing the computation cost significantly. However, we will still not get much information from random points. Using the whole information, we can get too much noise and lose the important parts of an object representation. Eventually, we need to consider that both ideas — getting all pixels and selecting random pixels — are really bad. So, what can we do instead?

Since we are working with a grayscale image and we need to get a unique point, we need to focus on intensity information, for example, getting object edges like we did with the Canny edge detector or Sobel filter. We are closer to the solution! But still, not close enough. What if we have a long edge? Don't you think that it is a bit bad that we have too many unique pixels which lay on this edge? An edge of an object has end points or corners. If we reduce our edge to those corners, we will get enough unique pixels and remove unnecessary information.

There are various methods of getting keypoints from an image, many of them extract corners as keypoints. To get them, we will use the **Features from Accelerated Segment Test (FAST)** algorithm. It is really simple and you can easily implement it by yourself if you want. But you do not need to. The algorithm implementation is provided both by the tracking.js and JSFeat libraries.

The idea of the FAST algorithm can be captured from the following image:

Suppose we want to check whether the pixel **P** is a corner, we will check 16 pixels around it. And if at least 9 pixels in an arc around **P** are much darker or brighter than the **P** value, then we say that **P** is a corner. How much darker or brighter the **P** pixels be? The decision is made by applying a threshold for the difference between the value of **P** and the value of pixels around **P**.

A practical example

First, we will start with an example of FAST corner detection for the tracking.js library. Before we do something, we can set the detector threshold. The threshold defines the minimum difference between a tested corner and points around it:

```
tracking.Fast.THRESHOLD = 30;
```

It is usually good practice to apply a Gaussian blur to an image before we start the method. It significantly reduces the noise of an image:

```
var imageData = context.getImageData(0, 0, cols, rows);
var gray = tracking.Image.grayscale(imageData.data, cols, rows, true);
var blurred4 = tracking.Image.blur(gray, cols, rows, 3);
```

Remember, that the blur function returns a 4 channel array—RGBA. In that case, we need to convert it to a 1-channel array. Since we can easily skip other channels, it should not be a problem:

```
var blurred1 = new Array(blurred4.length / 4);
for (var i = 0, j = 0; i < blurred4.length; i += 4, ++j) {
    blurred1[j] = blurred4[i];
}
```

Next, we run a corner detection function on our image array:

```
var corners = tracking.Fast.findCorners(blurred1, cols, rows);
```

The result returns an array where length is twice that of the corners number. The array is returned in a format: `[x0,y0,x1,y1,...]`, where `[xn, yn]` are coordinates of a detected corner. To print the result on a canvas, we will use the `fillRect` function. Since the number of points is usually around several hundreds, we cannot efficiently use `<div>` tag for that:

```
for (i = 0; i < corners.length; i += 2) {
    context.fillStyle = '#0f0';
    context.fillRect(corners[i], corners[i + 1], 3, 3);
}
```

Now we will see an example with the JSFeat library, the steps for which are very similar to what we saw with tracking.js. First, we set the global threshold with a function:

```
jsfeat.fast_corners.set_threshold(30);
```

Then, we apply a Gaussian blur to the image matrix and run corner detection:

```
jsfeat.imgproc.gaussian_blur(matGray, matBlurred, 3);
```

We need to preallocate keypoints for a corner's result. The `keypoint_t` function is just a new type, which is useful for key points of an image. The first two parameters represent coordinates of a point, and the other parameters represent point score (is that point good enough to be a key point?) point level (which you can use in an image pyramid, for example), and point angle (which is usually used for the gradient orientation):

```
var corners = [];
var i = cols * rows;
while (--i >= 0) {
    corners[i] = new jsfeat.keypoint_t(0, 0, 0, 0, -1);
}
```

After all this, we execute the FAST corner detection method. As a last parameter of the detection function, we define a border size. The border is used to constrain circles around each possible corner. For example, you cannot precisely say if the point is a corner for the `[0,0]` pixel. There is no `[0, -3]` pixel in our matrix:

```
var count = jsfeat.fast_corners.detect(matBlurred, corners, 3);
```

Since we preallocated the corners, the function returns the number of calculated corners for us. The result returns an array of structures with the x and y fields, so we can print it using those fields:

```
for (var i = 0; i < count; i++) {
    context.fillStyle = '#0f0';
    context.fillRect(corners[i].x, corners[i].y, 3, 3);
}
```

The result is nearly the same for both algorithms. The difference is in some parts of realization. Let's look at the following examples:

From left to right: tracking.js without blur, JSFeat without blur, tracking.js and JSFeat with blur.

If you look closely, you can see the difference between tracking.js and JSFeat results, but it is not easy to spot. Look at how much noise was reduced by applying just a small 3 x 3 Gaussian filter! A lot of noisy points were removed from the background. And now the algorithm can focus on points that represent flowers and the pattern of the vase.

We extracted key points from our image, and we successfully reached the goal of reducing the number of keypoints and focusing on the unique points of an image. Now we need to compare or match those points somehow. How we can do that? We will cover this in the next chapter.

Descriptors and object matching

Image features by themselves are a bit useless. Yes, we have found unique points on an image. But what did we get? Only pixels values and that's it. If we try to compare those values it will not give us much information. Moreover, if we change the overall image brightness, we will not find the same keypoints on the same image! Taking into account all of this, we need the information which surrounds our key points. Moreover, we need a method to efficiently compare this information. First, we need to describe the image features, which comes from image descriptors. In this part, we will see how those descriptors can be extracted and matched. The tracking.js and JSFeat libraries provide different methods for image descriptors. We will discuss both.

The BRIEF and ORB descriptors

The descriptors theory is focused on changes in an image pixels' intensities. The tracking.js library provides the **Binary Robust Independent Elementary Features (BRIEF)** descriptors and the its JSFeat extension **Oriented FAST and Rotated BRIEF (ORB)**. As we can see from the ORB naming, it is rotation invariant. This means that even if you rotate an object, the algorithm can still detect it. Moreover, the authors of the JSFeat library provide an example using the image pyramid, which is scale invariant too.

Let's start by explaining BRIEF, since it is the source for ORB descriptors. As a first step, the algorithm takes computed image features, and it takes the unique pairs of elements around each feature. Based on these pairs' intensities, it forms a binary string. For example, if we have a positions pair i and j, and if $I(i) < I(j)$ (where $I(pos)$ indicates the value of the image at the position pos), then the result is 1, otherwise 0. We add this result to the binary string. We do this for N pairs, where N is taken as a power of 2 $(128, 256, 512)$. Since descriptors are just binary strings, we can compare them in an efficient manner. To match these strings, the Hamming distance is usually used. It shows the minimum number of substitutions required to change one string to another. For example, if we have two binary strings— 10011 and 11001, the Hamming distance between them is 2, since we need to change two bits of information to change the first string to the second.

The JSFeat library provides the functionality to apply the ORB descriptors. The core idea is very similar to that of BRIEF. There are two major differences:

- The implementation is scale invariant, since the descriptors are computed for an image pyramid.

- The descriptors are rotation invariant; the direction is computed using intensity of the patch around a feature. Using this orientation, ORB manages to compute a BRIEF descriptor in a rotation invariant manner.

Descriptors implementation and their matching

Our goal is to find an object from a template on a scene image. We can do that by finding features and descriptors on both images and by matching descriptors from a template to an image.

We start from the tracking.js library and BRIEF descriptors. The first thing that you can do is set the number of location pairs:

```
tracking.Brief.N = 512
```

By default, it is 256, but you can choose a higher value. The larger the value the more information you will get and the more memory and computational cost it requires.

Before starting the computation, do not forget to apply the Gaussian blur. Next, we find the FAST corners and compute descriptors on both images. In the following code, we use the suffix Object for a template image and Scene for a scene image:

```
var cornersObject = tracking.Fast.findCorners(grayObject, colsObject,
rowsObject);
var cornersScene = tracking.Fast.findCorners(grayScene, colsScene,
rowsScene);
var descriptorsObject = tracking.Brief.getDescriptors(grayObject,
colsObject, cornersObject);
var descriptorsScene = tracking.Brief.getDescriptors(grayScene,
colsScene, cornersScene);
```

Then, we do the matching:

```
var matches = tracking.Brief.reciprocalMatch(cornersObject,
descriptorsObject, cornersScene, descriptorsScene);
```

We need to pass both the corners and descriptors information to the function, since it returns coordinate information as a result.

Next, we print both images on one canvas. To draw the matches using this trick, we need to shift our scene keypoints for the width of a template image. As a keypoint1 the matching function returns points on a template image and keypoint2 matched points from a scene image. The keypoint1/2 are arrays with x and y coordinates at 0 and 1 indexes, respectively:

```
for (var i = 0; i < matches.length; i++) {
    var color = '#' + Math.floor(Math.random() * 16777215).
toString(16);
    context.fillStyle = color;
    context.strokeStyle = color;
```

```
    context.fillRect(matches[i].keypoint1[0], matches[i].keypoint1[1],
5, 5);
    context.fillRect(matches[i].keypoint2[0] + colsObject, matches[i].
keypoint2[1], 5, 5);
    context.beginPath();
    context.moveTo(matches[i].keypoint1[0], matches[i].keypoint1[1]);
    context.lineTo(matches[i].keypoint2[0] + colsObject, matches[i].
keypoint2[1]);
    context.stroke();
}
```

The JSFeat library provides most of the code for pyramids and scale invariant features not in the library, but in the examples, which are available on `https://github.com/inspirit/jsfeat/blob/gh-pages/sample_orb.html`. We will not provide the full code here, because it requires too much space. But do not worry; we will highlight the main topics.

Let's start from functions that are included in the library. First, we need to preallocate the descriptors matrix, where 32 is the length of a descriptor and 500 is the maximum number of descriptors. Again 32 is a power of two:

```
var descriptors = new jsfeat.matrix_t(32, 500, jsfeat.U8C1_t);
```

Then, we compute the ORB descriptors for each corner, we need to do this for both template and scene images:

```
jsfeat.orb.describe(matBlurred, corners, num_corners, descriptors);
```

JSFeat does not provide a matching function in the library but it does in the examples section. The function uses global variables, which mainly define input descriptors and output matching:

```
function match_pattern()
```

The resulting `match_t` function contains the following fields:

- `screen_idx`: This is the index of a scene descriptor
- `pattern_lev`: This is the index of a pyramid level
- `pattern_idx`: This is the index of a template descriptor

Since ORB works with the image pyramid, it returns corners and matches for each level the pyramid:

```
var s_kp = screen_corners[m.screen_idx];
var p_kp = pattern_corners[m.pattern_lev][m.pattern_idx];
```

We can print each matching as follows. Again, we use *Shift*, since we computed descriptors on separate images, but print the result on one canvas:

```
context.fillRect(p_kp.x, p_kp.y, 4, 4);
context.fillRect(s_kp.x + shift, s_kp.y, 4, 4);
```

Finding an object location

We found a match. That is great. But what we did not do is find the object location. There is no function for that in the tracking.js library but JSFeat provides such a functionality in the examples section.

First, we need to compute a perspective transform matrix. Remember the first chapter? We have points from two images, but we do not have a transformation for the whole image.

First, we define a transform matrix:

```
var homo3x3 = new jsfeat.matrix_t(3, 3, jsfeat.F32C1_t);
```

To compute the homography, we need only four points. But after the matching, we get too many. In addition, there can be noisy points, which we want to skip somehow. For this, we use a **Random sample consensus (RANSAC)** algorithm. It is an iterative method for estimating a mathematical model from a dataset that contains outliers (noise). It estimates outliers and generates a model that is computed without the noisy data.

Before we start, we need to define the algorithm parameters. The first parameter is a match mask, where all matches will be marked as good (1) or bad (0).

```
var match_mask = new jsfeat.matrix_t(500, 1, jsfeat.U8C1_t);
```

Next parameter is a mathematical model which we want to obtain using the RANSAC algorithm:

```
var mm_kernel = new jsfeat.motion_model.homography2d();
```

Third, we need minimum number of points to estimate a model (4 points to get a homography), this can be defined as follows:

```
var num_model_points = 4;
```

Then, it is useful to have a maximum threshold to classify a data point as an inlier or a good match:

```
var reproj_threshold = 3;
```

Finally, the variable which holds the main parameters, that is, the last two arguments define the maximum ratio of outliers and probability of success. The algorithm stops when the number of inliers is 99 percent:

```
var ransac_param = new jsfeat.ransac_params_t(num_model_points,
        reproj_threshold, 0.5, 0.99);
```

Then we run the RANSAC algorithm. The last parameter represents the number of maximum iterations for the algorithm.

```
jsfeat.motion_estimator.ransac(ransac_param, mm_kernel,
        object_xy, screen_xy, count, homo3x3, match_mask, 1000);
```

The shape finding can be applied for both tracking.js and JSFeat libraries, you just need to set matches as `object_xy` and `screen_xy`, where those arguments must hold an array of objects with the x and y fields. After we find the transformation matrix, we compute the projected shape of an object to a new image:

```
var shape_pts = tCorners(homo3x3.data, colsObject, rowsObject);
```

After the computation is done, we draw the computed shapes on our images:

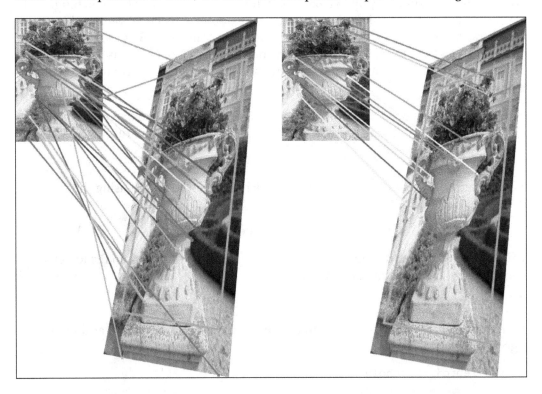

As we see, our program successfully found an object in both cases. Actually, both methods can show different performance, it is mainly based on the thresholds you set.

Summary

We completed one of the hardest chapters in this book. Congratulations! We saw how to find and track a basic colored object and plunged into the depths of library APIs. Oh, and don't forget, we have completed our own object detector! The applications of Computer Vision methods vary. What we cannot accomplish with the simple color detection, we achieve with powerful feature detection and descriptor matching algorithms. Both libraries provide different functionalities to match the objects and some functions are not included in the libraries. But it should not stop you from using those excellent methods. To know how and, probably the more important part, when to use those algorithms are the most crucial things you need to know.

One of the most commonly seen objects in our world is a person's face. We interact with people everywhere. However, we did not see how to detect such objects in an application. The algorithms we covered in this chapter are not so useful for face detection, which is why we need to introduce new methods for that. This is our topic of the next chapter. See you there!

4
Smile and Wave, Your Face Has Been Tracked!

The most commonly seen object in our lives is a human face. We interact with people everywhere even when we do not meet them in person; we write a lot of messages via social networks, such as Twitter and Facebook, or e-mails and text messages using our phones. Face detection and tracking has many applications. In some cases, you might want to create a human computer interface, which will take the head position as an input or, more likely, you might want to help your users with tagging their friends. Actually, there are a lot of face detection libraries, which are written on JavaScript; these outnumber the libraries that focus on image processing itself. This is a good opportunity to choose the library that you really need. In addition to face detection, many libraries support face particle recognition and recognition of other objects.

In this chapter, we will focus on the JSFeat (`http://inspirit.github.io/jsfeat/`), tracking.js (`http://inspirit.github.io/jsfeat/`), and headtrackr (`https://github.com/auduno/headtrackr`) libraries. The last library supports head tracking instead of just recognition. Most of the libraries focus on Haar-like features detection.

With the help of several examples, we will cover the following topics in this chapter:

- Face detection with JSFeat
- Tagging people with tracking.js
- Head tracking with Camshift

Face detection with JSFeat

We saw detection of various objects in the previous chapter. The human face is much more complicated than just a regular color object, for example. More complex detectors share in common such things like the usage of brightness information and the patterns that this information forms. First of all, we need to see how face recognition is done. Without that, the tracking process will be quite difficult to understand. Actually, in most cases, the face recognition part is just the first step of face tracking algorithms.

We start with the JSFeat project. This awesome library provides a functionality to detect a face in two ways. Both have many applications in the real world. We will see how both of them work from the inside and discuss the API provided by JSFeat.

Face detection using Haar-like features

This is probably the most popular face detector nowadays. Most of the libraries use exactly this algorithm as a common face detector. It is easy to implement and use. In addition to this, it can be used in any application as it gives good precision in face detection. The method itself forms a Viola-Jones object detection framework, which was proposed by Paul Viola and Michael Jones in 2001.

Remember the convolution kernels from *Chapter 2, Turn Your Browser into Photoshop*? Take a look at this picture:

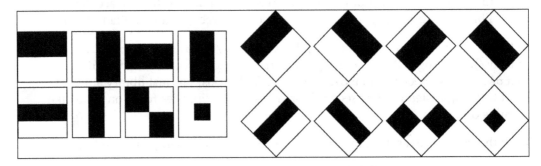

The rectangles are called Haar-like features or Haar features. They are just convolution kernels, where we subtract pixels under the white rectangle and add pixels where under the black part. To compute them fast, we use integral images. If you do not remember the concept, then you had better refresh your memory by referring to the section on integral image under the section *What is filtering and how to use it* in *Chapter 2, Turn Your Browser into Photoshop*. Briefly, the integral image provides substantial support in fast calculation of the sum of pixels in a rectangular area of an image.

We can use the features shown in the right-hand side of the picture too. They are rotated by 45 degrees. For that case, we use the tilted integral. They can capture more object details. The functionality for tilted features is available in most of the libraries. But there is a problem which prevents its usage in real-world applications — the Haar features are usually applied on low resolution parts of an image, for example, 20 x 20 or 24 x 24; when we rotate a feature (or integral image), we may face rounding errors. Because of this, those features are rarely used in practice.

How can these features help us? Using them, we can describe an object by selecting the unique features of it. For example, you see an ordinary female face under low resolution in the following images:

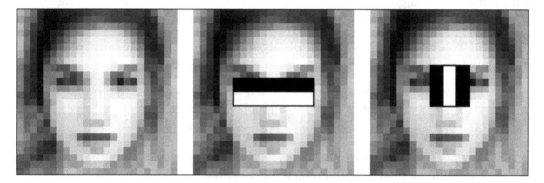

Usually, the part with the eyes is darker than the lower part. Furthermore, the nose is brighter than the eyes and the brows. We already found two unique face features!

For the input image, we use a sliding window to apply those kernels and check whether an object in the window is a face or not. We need to do this for all possible sizes and locations of kernels, which is practically impossible. Even for a 24 x 24 window, we need to check more than 160,000 features. Of course, there is a solution for this. We need to train a classifier and save only those features that are relevant to the detected object, in our case, it is a face. Unfortunately, JavaScript libraries do not provide such a functionality. Actually, they do not need to do so, since the libraries we use already contain most of necessary classifiers for face detection. Besides, the training time can take from several hours to months. However, if you need to detect something else or improve the detection accuracy, then you will probably want to see other libraries, for example, OpenCV (http://opencv.org). They provide the functionality to train your own classifier.

In short, during the training process, the algorithm checks all possible sizes and positions for features and selects the best of them that describe the object. After the first step we get several thousands of features. Still, this is too much. The next step provides a solution for this problem. We group these features into different stages of the classifier. When the algorithm checks the slide window, the algorithm evaluates it on each group one-by-one. If the first group fails the checking, then we discard that window and move on to another. This whole process structure is called a **Cascade of classifiers**. Eventually, the training process significantly reduces the number of features that need checking.

To make the algorithm scale invariant, it is applied using various window sizes. Unfortunately, the algorithm is not rotation invariant. You can try to apply this by rotating the source image but in that case, you may face incorrect results.

Now, you have an idea of how the whole algorithm works. Let's see how we can apply it in the JSFeat library by performing the following steps:

1. First, we need to define an object which we want to detect. In our case it is a face. To set an object, we need to add a JavaScript file:

   ```
   <script src="/path/to/frontalface.js"></script>
   ```

2. Then, set the classifier in the code. It contains cascades, the original window size, and the tilted integral flag, if it is required:

   ```
   var classifier = jsfeat.haar.frontalface;
   ```

3. Next, we get the image data from the context:

   ```
   var imageData = context.getImageData(0, 0, cols, rows);
   ```

4. We then define an image and convert it to grayscale:

   ```
   var mat = new jsfeat.matrix_t(cols, rows, jsfeat.U8C1_t);
   jsfeat.imgproc.grayscale(imageData.data, cols, rows, mat);
   ```

5. Sometimes, it is a good choice to increase the image contrast and remove some noise, which can be done as follows:

   ```
   jsfeat.imgproc.equalize_histogram(mat, mat);
   jsfeat.imgproc.gaussian_blur(mat, mat, 3);
   ```

6. We then predefine arrays for integrals:

   ```
   var integralSum = new Int32Array((cols + 1) * (rows + 1));
   var integralSqSum = new Int32Array((cols + 1) * (rows + 1));
   var integralTilted = new Int32Array((cols + 1) * (rows + 1));
   jsfeat.imgproc.compute_integral_image(mat, integralSum,
   integralSqSum, classifier.tilted ? integralTilted : null);
   ```

7. Take a close look at what we do here. We compute the tilted integral only if it is set to `true` in the classifier. There is a part that is not required, but in some cases, it helps to speed up the computation and remove noisy elements. We will check the edges' density using the Canny edge detector and its integral:

```
var integralCanny = new Int32Array((cols + 1) * (rows + 1));
var edges = new jsfeat.matrix_t(cols, rows, jsfeat.U8C1_t);
jsfeat.imgproc.canny(mat, edges, 10, 50);
jsfeat.imgproc.compute_integral_image(edges, integralCanny, null,
null);
```

8. If the number of edges in a window is less than the edges' density. Then the program will skip that window without checking the Haar features. You can set the density threshold in JSFeat as follows:

```
jsfeat.haar.edges_density = 0.13;
```

9. Next, we set the other parameters and call the function:

```
var minScale = 2;
var scaleFactor = 1.1;
var bb = jsfeat.haar.detect_multi_scale(integralSum,
integralSqSum, integralTilted, integralCanny,
        mat.cols, mat.rows, classifier, scaleFactor, minScale);
```

If you look into the frontalface.js file, you will see that the original window size is 20 x 20 pixels, but we set the `minScale` variable in the preceding code block assuming that there will be no face that is smaller than 40x40 pixels. The `scaleFactor` variable is the factor for the scale. The process stops when the window increases to the image size.

The algorithm returns multiple rectangles for each face. Why? Because when the algorithm moves the window, the movement can be too small to make a big difference to the image. The JSFeat library provides a method to group those rectangles, where the last parameter indicates how many neighbors the result should have in order to be grouped with another one:

```
bb = jsfeat.haar.group_rectangles(bb, 1);
```

Moreover, the algorithm returns confidence for each detection, and if we want to print only the best detections, then we can sort the result array and print only the most confident ones:

```
jsfeat.math.qsort(bb, 0, bb.length - 1, function (a, b) {
    return (b.confidence < a.confidence);
});
for (var i = 0; i < maxFaceNumber; ++i) {
    var b = bb[i];
    context.strokeStyle = "#fff";
    context.strokeRect(b.x, b.y, b.width, b.height);
}
```

After applying this to an image, we get the following result:

On the first image, we painted all rectangles without grouping; see how many detections we got for the faces? The different sizes represent different window scales. On the second image, we painted the faces after grouping. Already good enough, isn't it? And for the last one, we chose the four most confident detections.

As we can see, the algorithm has many interesting parts and it really helps to detect faces on photos. There are various implementations of that algorithm. In addition, this method has many extensions. We will discuss one of them in the next section.

Brightness binary features

From the section name, you may conclude that this method works with a change in image brightness, probably with its pixels, and that it compares those intensity values to receive some sort of a binary check. You are totally right! In some ways, it is like getting FAST corners, but the whole idea is a bit more complex. Let's discuss it.

The main difference between brightness binary features and Haar features is that it uses distinct pixels instead of convolutions. Moreover, it uses different image pyramids not different sliding window sizes to compute the required features.

You can get an idea from the following image:

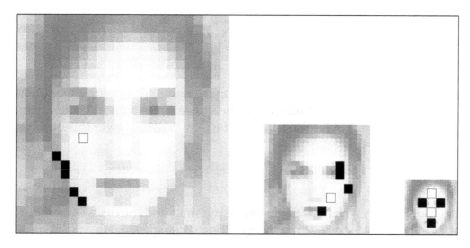

We kept the resolution of all three images the same for a better view. But you need to keep in mind that the images are 24x24, 12x12, and 6x6 pixels. Besides, white and black points represent pixels.

Here, the idea is very similar to what you saw while learning the Haar features. For example, eyes are much darker than other face particles and because of that, we indicate them as dark or black points. The correct instance of an object must follow the rules: all white points i and black points j in a window should satisfy the expression `I(i) > I(j)`, where `I(position)` is a pixel value of a window at this position.

The number of points may vary, it is chosen during the classifier training process. The format for the classifier is different from the format of the Haar features. The training process is much more complex, since it needs to get various point combinations. In case you want to train your own classifier, you may want to follow the CCV library (`http://libccv.org/doc/doc-bbf/`). This is a C library that provides implementations of various Computer Vision algorithms.

It is harder to find a BBF algorithm implementation, since it is more complicated and the training process is much more difficult. Also, the JSFeat library provides the algorithm for the same. First, you need to include the classifier file:

```
<script src="/path/to/bbf_face.js"></script>
```

Then, you need to preallocate some data before the computation starts:

```
jsfeat.bbf.prepare_cascade(jsfeat.bbf.face_cascade);
```

As usual, we work with grayscale images; we get one using the standard JSFeat functions:

```
var imageData = context.getImageData(0, 0, cols, rows);
var mat = new jsfeat.matrix_t(cols, rows, jsfeat.U8C1_t);
jsfeat.imgproc.grayscale(imageData.data, cols, rows, mat);
```

One of the important steps is generating an image pyramid. The input parameters are: input image, minimum dimensions of the image in the pyramid, and an interval. It sets the number of original scale levels in the pyramid; the larger this number, the more pyramid levels you get:

```
var pyramid = jsfeat.bbf.build_pyramid(mat, minWidth, minHeight,
interval);
```

Then call the function which takes the image pyramid and the cascade as input parameters. After all this, we group the resulting rectangles together:

```
var bb = jsfeat.bbf.detect(pyramid, jsfeat.bbf.face_cascade);
bb = jsfeat.bbf.group_rectangles(bb, 1);
```

Here is the result we get with our image:

For the first part, we took the result without rectangle grouping and for the second, with it. As for the Haar features, you may select only the most confident results.

In the preceding image, we see that the result performed poorly compared to the Haar features. It is hard to say why it gives such result. In many cases, it highly depends on the implementation or classifier training or maybe just on the input image.

We saw two different algorithms, you can select one by your choice. It is probably better to stay with the Haar features, since you will find a lot of realizations of that algorithm. In contrast, if you want to extend the Computer Vision practical boundaries, you may want to tune the BBF implementation or just write your own. It is all in your hands!

Tagging people with tracking.js

To see more about Haar-like features and its implementation, we will discuss tracking.js library. It provides nearly the same functionality as the JSFeat library. What is interesting is that it supplies classifiers for other different objects, for example, face particles. Eventually, we will see how to make it possible to tag friends.

Haar features with tracking.js

Tracking.js provides the functionality to detect not only a face, but various face particles too. It is very easy to do that. You need to perform the following steps:

1. First, you need to add object files for what you want to detect:

   ```
   <script src="/path/to/face.js"></script>
   <script src="/path/to/eye.js"></script>
   <script src="/path/to/mouth.js"></script>
   ```

2. Next, initialize the `ObjectTracker` function. We did not discuss this in the previous chapter, since it is mostly focused on face detection, not just a regular object. Anyway, we initialize it with the names of the objects we want to track:

   ```
   var tracker = new tracking.ObjectTracker(['face', 'eye', 'mouth']);
   ```

3. There are also custom functions that you can call. One of them is the `setStepSize` function, which sets the step size for a sliding window or how it is called in the tracking.js library block:

   ```
   tracker.setStepSize(1.2);
   ```

4. We then define the postprocessing function. What we need is to plot our result on a canvas:

   ```
   tracker.on('track', function (event) {
       event.data.forEach(function (rect) {
           plot(rect.x, rect.y, rect.width, rect.height);
       });
   });
   ```

We also need the `plot` function itself:

```
var canvas = document.getElementById('initCanvas');
var context = canvas.getContext('2d');
function plot(x, y, w, h) {
    context.lineWidth = 3;
    context.globalAlpha = 0.8;
    context.strokeStyle = "#fff";
    context.strokeRect(x, y, w, h);
}
```

As we mentioned, there is no functionality to plot different objects with distinct colors. For now, you can operate with different objects by creating several different trackers at once. Eventually, the last thing you need to do is to call the `track` function on a canvas:

```
tracking.track('#initCanvas', tracker);
```

There are various functions that you can use:

- `setEdgesDensity`: This is the same as in the JSFeat library, you just set a threshold for a sliding window edge's density. It may significantly improve the result; the higher the value, the more edges a window needs to contain to be a candidate for an object we want to find.

- `setInitialScale`: This is the initial scale for a sliding window.

- `setScaleFactor`: This is the scale factor for the sliding window.

Using these functions, you can tune the algorithm a bit to get a better result.

We tested the algorithm by applying three detectors one-by-one. For the face, eye, and mouth we used red, blue, and green colors, respectively. Here is the result:

As you can see, the result for faces is much better than those for face particles. This can be due to the bad lighting conditions or poorly trained classifier.

Tagging people in photos

Tagging people in photos is a common procedure that you use a lot in social networks. If you want to create similar functionality on your website, the JavaScript world can offer something for you. Actually, you can do that with any library which provides face detection methods, you just need to write some additional methods. To simplify the code, we will follow an example from the tracking.js library. It is easy to understand and implement:

1. First, we need to place our image to the HTML code:

    ```
    <div id="photo"><img id="img" src="/path/to/your/image.jpg"/></div>
    ```

2. Here is an array that holds all the names that need to be tagged:

    ```
    var theBeatles = ['George Harrison', 'John Lennon', 'Ringo Starr', 'Paul McCartney'];
    ```

3. Then, we start from initializing our `ObjectTracker` function with a `face` object:

    ```
    var tracker = new tracking.ObjectTracker('face');
    ```

4. The whole magic goes on in a post processing function:

    ```
    tracker.on('track', function (event) {
        var data = event.data;
        data.sort(function (a, b) {
            return b.x - a.x;
        });
        data = data.filter(function (el) {
            return el.width >= 50;
        });
        data.forEach(function (rect) {
            tag(rect.x, rect.y, rect.width, rect.height);
        });
    });
    ```

5. Let's review it a bit. First, we sort all rectangles by x coordinates, it will be much easier to plot the result when we know the order of detections.

6. Next, we filter our object array and skip all detections in which width is less then must be "50" pixels. That will help us to omit background or noisy detections. Moreover, we present a new `tag` function, which will tag all detections on a photo. See the following code:

```
var img = document.getElementById('img');
var tag = function (x, y, w, h) {
    var rect = document.createElement('div');
    var input = document.createElement('input');

    input.value = theBeatles.pop();
    rect.appendChild(input);
    imageContainer.appendChild(rect);
    rect.style.width = w + 'px';
    rect.style.height = h + 'px';
    rect.style.left = (img.offsetLeft + x) + 'px';
    rect.style.top = (img.offsetTop + y) + 'px';
    rect.style.position = 'absolute';
    rect.style.border = '3px solid white';
};
```

The function creates an `<input>` tag for a name, then takes the first element of an array and appends the input element to the `<div>` rectangle.

7. The last thing we need to do is to call our tracker on an image:

```
tracking.track(img, tracker);
```

Here is the result:

As you can see, we have successfully removed the background detection and tagged all four people in the correct order.

Head tracking with Camshift

Head tracking is another huge topic in the field of Computer Vision. It is very useful when you want to create a human computer interface. For example, it is usually used in web browser games to move objects or control a 3D interface. There are differences between object detection and tracking. First of all, tracking works only on videos, since you track an object (not reestimate) a new instance in each frame. Consequently, we need to assume that the object we track is the same as it was on the previous frame.

Tracking can be done for multiple objects but here we will focus on a single object, in our case, it is a head or more precisely — face. There is a wonderful library that can help us to track it. It is called headtrackr (`https://github.com/auduno/headtrackr`). In addition to face tracking, it provides a functionality to create an interface that helps to control your browser applications using head motion. We will not focus on the motion estimation part here, since the chapter is focused on face detection and tracking. But do not worry, we will get to that in the next chapter. First, we will see how the tracking algorithm works and then we will focus on its practical examples.

The idea behind head tracking

There are many object tracking algorithms but most of them are not suitable for JavaScript and web browsers due to computational complexity. For Haar features, it is very difficult to apply them in a rotation-invariant manner because when you do that for several skewed images, the algorithm becomes non-real time. The headtrackr library tends to solve that problem. It introduces a framework that can help you to track a face. Its main focus is creating a human interface, but it provides enough flexibility to use it for other tasks as well.

How does the tracking work? Suppose you have found an object on an initial frame, for example, using Haar features or another method. We can work with a video file or just a webcam. In that case, the difference between neighboring frames will not be that huge. These are our core assumptions, let's move on.

We will talk here about objects, not just a face. Let's assume that our object is a group of points and we want to find that group on the next frame. Look at the following image:

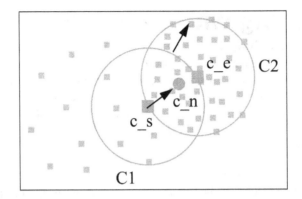

The circle (window) **C1** is the location of an object on a previous frame. The circle **C2** binds the group of points that we want to find. f we get a sum of them in the **C2** circle by adding the x and y coordinates and dividing their sums by the number of points in that circle, we will get point **c_n**, which is called **centroid**. After you find the centroid, we move the start circle center **c_s** to the new center **c_n**. The algorithm continues the iterating process by finding a new centroid until it converges in the end center **c_e**. You have found the position of our object on a new frame! This algorithm of finding centers of point densities is called **Meanshift**.

How can we get the density for the Meanshift algorithm when we use a face? The common approach is to generate a skin map, as shown in the following image:

In the right-hand side image, each pixel represents the probability of this pixel being a skin point. Let's call it a density picture. We get a centroid location using these intensity points in a window.

Can you see a problem with the Meanshift approach? We are not changing the size of a window. What if an object gets closer or further from the camera? We need to adapt the size of an object somehow. This issue was solved by the **CAMshift (Continuously Adaptive Meanshift)** algorithm. The first stage of the algorithm is the Meanshift approach. When we find the window with the highest density, the Camshift algorithm updates the window size based on the sum of the intensity values in that window. The higher the intensity and the more nonzero points in a window, the larger the output size will be. After all, the window converges to the required object. Moreover, the algorithm provides computation of a possible head rotation using the density picture.

See the following image:

The first one shows the original rectangle (the smaller one) and the final detection by Camshift. The right-hand side image shows the result after the rectangle angle calculation.

The headtrackr library can initialize the Meanshift algorithm in two ways:

- The user manually selects an object on a video and the tracking is done using the user input
- The algorithm can use Haar features to detect the face to be tracked

We will see an example with the second approach, when a face is detected automatically for the first frame using Haar features, and for the other frames, the library uses the Camshift approach.

The head tracking application

It is relatively easy to use the headtrackr library. It provides a flexible way to create a head tracking application. We will discuss the APIs and opportunities it provides:

1. The first thing we need to do is to add a headtrackr script. The Haar detector is already included there:

   ```
   <script src="js/headtrackr.js"></script>
   ```

2. Next, we need to define HTML inputs so that we can easily display the content:

   ```
   <canvas id="buffer" width="320" height="240"
   style="display:none"></canvas>
   <video id="inputVideo" autoplay loop width="320" height="240"></
   video>
   <canvas id="overlay" width="320" height="240"></canvas>
   <canvas id="debug" width="320" height="240"></canvas>
   ```

   The first one will hold the data required for the library. The video file will hold the video. The other two tags are optional, the third one provides a canvas to draw the tracking result rectangle on it. The last is used to display the density image.

3. If you want, you can add a tag for the headtrackr output text, which will display various messages during the working process, so you can understand the stage at which the tracker is:

   ```
   <span id='headtrackerMessage'></span>
   ```

4. After that, we need to get all the necessary data on the JavaScript side:

   ```
   var canvasInput = document.getElementById('buffer');
   var videoInput = document.getElementById('inputVideo');
   var canvasOverlay = document.getElementById('overlay');
   var overlayContext = canvasOverlay.getContext('2d');
   var debugOverlay = document.getElementById('debug');
   canvasOverlay.style.position = "absolute";
   canvasOverlay.style.top = '0px';
   canvasOverlay.style.zIndex = '100001';
   canvasOverlay.style.display = 'block';
   ```

   The canvas should be above the video, so we set its style to be so.

5. Next, you need to initialize tracker parameters:

```
var htracker = new headtrackr.Tracker({
    altVideo: {webm: "/path/to/your/video.webm"},
    calcAngles: true,
    ui: true,
    debug: debugOverlay
});
```

There are a lot of parameters, we will focus on those which are useful in this example. By default, the headtrackr library works with a web camera. If you do not have one or your browser does not support it, you can provide a video file using the `altVideo` parameter. To calculate the head angle, we use the `calcAngles` variable, which is `false` by default. The `ui` parameter sets debugging messages for a tag with the `headtrackerMessage` id. For a density image, we need to set the `debug` parameter.

6. Next, we init the tracker with a video and canvas inputs. Then, we start the tracker:

```
htracker.init(videoInput, canvasInput);
htracker.start();
```

7. To stop the tracking process, you can use the `stop` function. In that case, the library will reinitiate the whole process:

```
htracker.stop();
```

8. To display the result using overlay, we need to add a listener to the `facetrackingEvent`. Besides, you can see how we get the rotated version of a rectangle:

```
document.addEventListener("facetrackingEvent", function (event) {
    overlayContext.clearRect(0, 0, 320, 240);
    if (event.detection == "CS") {
        overlayContext.translate(event.x, event.y);
        overlayContext.rotate(event.angle - (Math.PI / 2));
        overlayContext.strokeStyle = "#00CC00";
        overlayContext.strokeRect((-event.width / 2) >> 0,
(-event.height / 2) >> 0, event.width, event.height);
        overlayContext.rotate((Math.PI / 2) - event.angle);
        overlayContext.translate(-event.x, -event.y);
    }
});
```

The result includes a video with the overlay over it and the debug information on the right:

As you can see, there is nothing difficult in applying the head tracking with that library. To use the library in a proper manner, you just need to know some parts of the algorithm.

Summary

A face is a really complex object. To detect and track it, you need to use a new level of algorithms. Fortunately, the JavaScript libraries provide such an opportunity through Haar, Brightness Binary features, Meanshift, and Camshift algorithms. All of them have their own area of usage. You can apply these wonderful methods in different programs, for example, people tagging. We discussed them and provided examples which you can start using right away. In addition to face detection, there is a potential to detect other objects such as face particles. Of course, the detection quality may vary significantly and you should be careful when you use other classifiers.

In this chapter, we already touched on the tracking applications a bit and discussed how the tracking can help to create a human interface. In the next chapter, we will learn how to control your browser with motion and how the object tracking can be used in those applications.

5
May JS Be with You! Control Your Browser with Motion

Imagine how exciting it would be to be able to control your browser using neither the keyboard nor mouse. There are many fields in computer science that tend to create a good human interface. One of those fields is Computer Vision. It provides outstanding methods that can help you to create something useful rapidly and you do not even need devices such as Kinect! The human interface in Computer Vision highly depends on object tracking. In the previous chapter, we already saw some object tracking examples, such as Camshift. Here, we will introduce more algorithms to play with. First, we will start with the basic tracking algorithms, which do not have any assumptions about an object from a previous frame. Next, we will move on to **Head-coupled perspective**; this is a technique that uses the head (or eye) position to simulate a 3D environment on a screen. This will be covered by the headtrackr library, which we have seen in the previous chapter (`https://github.com/auduno/headtrackr`). Finally, we will move on to the optical flow algorithms, with the help of which you can track many different objects in your application and even create programs which can be controlled by gestures. We will create an interesting example that uses that type of control. Here, we will introduce a new library (`https://github.com/anvaka/oflow`), which provides an excellent way to generate the optical flow of an image. To track multiple points at once, we will use the JSFeat (`http://inspirit.github.io/jsfeat/`) library. Let's get started!

We will cover the following topics in this chapter:

- Basic tracking with tracking.js
- Controlling objects with head motion
- Optical flow for motion estimation

Basic tracking with tracking.js

In this section, we will refresh our knowledge about object detection and create a sample project, which will show how object detection can be presented as object tracking. This is a relatively simple topic but, in some cases, it can outperform other methods. Remember that object detection deals with detecting instances of objects, while tracking deals with locating moving objects over time. If you have only one unique object and you assume it will still be unique on the next frames, then you can calculate its location over time. In that case, we do not need to worry about tracking techniques because the tracking can be done using object detection. Here, we will focus mostly on the tracking.js library (`http://trackingjs.com`) since it provides the easiest way to do that.

An example of an object tracking application

We already mentioned the idea of using object detection as tracking. The idea is using a unique object on a scene. This can be a colored ball, your head, hand, or anything that has something special and can help to distinguish it from other objects in a scene. When you have that object, you just detect it on a frame and calculate its centroid to get its position.

To explore this concept, we will use the tracking.js library. We will draw a small ball with its center at the centroid of the detected object.

First, we will place the necessary tags for a video and the ball scene:

```
<video id='video' width='640' height='480' preload autoplay>
    <source src="/path/to/your/video.mp4">
</video>
<canvas id='ballCanvas' width='640px' height='480px'></canvas>
```

We need to get the ball's context and its parameters to be able to draw on it:

```
var ballCanvas = document.getElementById('ballCanvas'),
        ballContext = ballCanvas.getContext('2d'),
        ballSceneW = ballCanvas.width,
        ballSceneH = ballCanvas.height;
```

The object we want to track is just a simple colored object, so we will use `ColorTracker`. To remove noise, we set the minimum dimensions of a detected object to `20`:

```
var tracker = new tracking.ColorTracker(['yellow']);
tracker.setMinDimension(20);
```

When we detect an object, we need to clear the context that contains the ball. In addition, we take the first detected object and use it to move the ball to a new position:

```
tracker.on('track', function (event) {
    ballContext.clearRect(0, 0, ballSceneW, ballSceneH);
    if (event.data.length > 0)
        move(event.data[0]);
});
```

The move function is defined in the following code:

```
function move(rect) {
    ballContext.beginPath();
    var ballX = rect.x + rect.width / 2;
    var ballY = rect.y + rect.height / 2;
    ballContext.arc(ballX, ballY, 30, 0, 2 * Math.PI, false);
    ballContext.fillStyle = 'yellow';
    ballContext.fill();
    ballContext.stroke();
}
```

As we can see, we take the center of a detected rectangle and draw a ball using it.

To start the tracker, we just initiate it using the track function on the `<video>` tag:

```
tracking.track('#video', tracker);
```

Here, we did not place the code for displaying the tracked object on a video because we already covered it in *Chapter 3, Easy Object Detection for Everyone*.

Here is what we get:

The preceding image shows the detection of a bird in different frames and the estimated positions of the corresponding ball below the detections. As we can see, our main assumption about the object's (bird) uniqueness is observed. The only question is about the tracking—the bird's head is not perfectly detected.

We saw the basic object detection, which is one step closer to tracking but it is not 100 percent. What we need to do is to remember the old coordinates of a previous object position and compute the motion vector. Let's move on!

Controlling objects with the head motion

Creating a human interface in Computer Vision is not an easy task. One of the exciting fields is Head-coupled perspective. This technique is used for rendering the scene on the screen, which responds naturally to changes in the head position of a viewer relative to the display. Simply put, the technology creates a 3D display without using any additional devices except the camera.

In the previous chapter, we saw how to track a head with the headtrackr library. It was done using the Camshift algorithm. In this section, we will explain the background of the function for Head-coupled perspective and how to use it in your projects to create an amazing human interface. To present a scene, the headtrackr library uses one of the most popular JavaScript libraries for 3D modeling—three.js (`http://threejs.org`). We will begin with an explanation of the core function and then see an example of its usage.

The Head-coupled perspective

As we mentioned earlier, the headtrackr library works with three.js. The three.js library provides a clear API and exceptional functionality for 3D modeling. If you want, you can switch to another library, but in that case, you will need to rewrite some code from the headtrackr library.

The headtrackr library provides a good explanation of the whole algorithm; you can refer to it at `http://auduno.com/post/25125149521/head-tracking-with-webrtc`. To help you better understand the whole process, and in case you want to modify the functionality of the head tracking or use other libraries for the 3D modeling, here we will focus on the code of the core function.

The function itself is called:

```
headtrackr.controllers.three.realisticAbsoluteCameraControl
```

To change the perspective of a scene appropriately, we need to know the movement of a head in three directions: X, Y, and Z. To do this, we need to assume some scene attributes. The core assumption this method makes is that, at the first initialization of the algorithm, the distance between the user who sits in front of the screen and the camera is 60cm. In addition to this, the method defines the screen height, which is 20cm by default. Using these parameters, we can find the **Field of View** (**fov**):

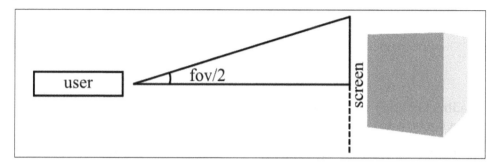

In the scene, we will create a camera that will represent a user (your head); we will call it **camera on a scene**. Do not confuse it with the camera that is used to capture your face, for example, the laptop's camera.

The bigger the fov angle, the more objects fit on a screen and the further they appear to be. The Fov is computed in the first frame where a head is detected, taking into account previously mentioned assumptions.

There are several parameters that the headtrackr function uses:

- **camera**: This is the `PerspectiveCamera` object from the three.js library.
- **scaling**: This is the vertical size of a screen in a 3D model. Basically, it scales the whole scene by the constant you define.
- **fixedPosition**: This is the initial position of a scene camera.
- **lookAt**: This is the position of the object you look at, which should be THREE.Vector3 which contains the 3 coordinates of an object.
- **params**: This includes a `screenHeight` field in centimeters. This is an optional parameter and it defines the height of your monitor.

During the algorithm initialization, first, we set the scene camera position and the position of the object that this camera should point at:

```
camera.position.x = fixedPosition[0];
camera.position.y = fixedPosition[1];
camera.position.z = fixedPosition[2];
camera.lookAt(lookAt);
```

Next, we define the screen width and height using the camera aspect ratio and scaling parameters:

```
var wh = screenHeight_cms * scaling;
var ww = wh * camera.aspect;
```

To get a head position in each frame, we need to add a listener to `headtrackingEvent`:

```
document.addEventListener('headtrackingEvent', function (event) {
...
// function body
...
});
```

The headtrackr library returns an estimated position of a head in each frame. The event contains the x, y, and z fields.

Since our camera represents our head position, to update its parameters, we need to change the position of the camera with respect to event data; do not forget about scaling:

```
camera.position.x = fixedPosition[0] + event.x * scaling;
camera.position.y = fixedPosition[1] + event.y * scaling;
camera.position.z = fixedPosition[2] + event.z * scaling;
```

You need to keep an object in the center of the screen. To do so, the method sets the view offset using the `setViewOffset` method. The first two parameters define the size of the whole view, the last four parameters are the parameters of a view rectangle:

```
var xOffset = event.x > 0 ? 0 : -event.x * 2 * scaling;
var yOffset = event.y < 0 ? 0 : event.y * 2 * scaling;
camera.setViewOffset(ww + Math.abs(event.x * 2 * scaling), wh + Math.
abs(event.y * 2 * scaling), xOffset, yOffset, ww, wh);
```

The last attribute we want to update is the field of view, for which we use the `atan2` function. It returns the result from `-PI` to `PI` in radians; we need to convert it to degrees and multiply it by 2, since we use only half of a screen in our computation:

```
camera.fov = Math.atan2(wh / 2 + Math.abs(event.y * scaling), Math.
abs(event.z * scaling)) * 180 * 2 / Math.PI;
```

After this, we update the camera parameters:

```
camera.updateProjectionMatrix();
```

As we saw, all we need to do is to work with the scene camera. If you want modify the code or use another library, it should not be a problem for you now.

Controlling a simple box

The example which is provided by the headtrackr library uses an old version of three.js but the good point is that it can be applied to new versions too! We will follow the cube example, which is available at `http://threejs.org/examples/#canvas_geometry_cube`. You can copy and paste the whole code from there; we will do only basic modifications.

First, you need to update the scripts section and add the headtrackr library:

```
<script src="js/three.min.js"></script>
<script src="js/Projector.js"></script>
<script src="js/CanvasRenderer.js"></script>
<script src="js/headtrackr.js"></script>
```

To track your face, you will need to define the video and canvas tags, which will be used by the headtrackr library:

```
<canvas id="compare" width="320" height="240" style="display:none"></canvas>
<video id="vid" autoplay loop></video>
```

Far plane of a scene camera in the three.js example is too close for us, we better set it a bit further away:

```
camera.far = 10000;
```

Initialization of the tracking process is done by the function that we reviewed in the previous section; take a look at the third parameter of a function below - camera position. The cube location in the example is `[0, 150, 0]` and its dimensions are 200 pixels. We set the camera initialization position at the cube plane:

```
headtrackr.controllers.three.realisticAbsoluteCameraControl(camera,
20, [0, 150, 100], cube.position);
```

Next, we create a tracker:

```
var htracker = new headtrackr.Tracker();
```

In the previous section, we reviewed the parameters that can be used while you track a face. Now, let's see what you can use for the head position estimation:

- **cameraOffset**: This is the distance from your laptop camera to the center of a screen, which is 11.5cm (half of the height of a regular laptop screen) by default.
- **fov**: This is the horizontal field of view used by the camera in degrees. By default, the algorithm automatically estimates this.

Now, we get the video and canvas on the JavaScript side. Then, we get the initialization and start the tracker:

```
var videoInput = document.getElementById('vid');
var canvasInput = document.getElementById('compare');
videoInput.style.position = 'absolute';
videoInput.style.top = '50px';
videoInput.style.zIndex = '100001';
videoInput.style.display = 'block';
htracker.init(videoInput, canvasInput);
htracker.start();
```

Here is a rough sketch of what you will see while using the application:

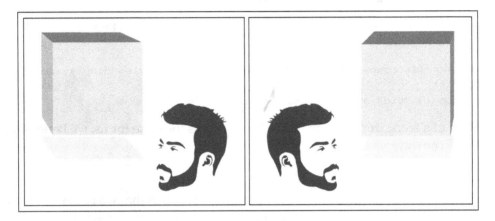

Keep in mind that when you move your head to the left, the camera will display the movement to the right. You can move your head in any direction, the only issue with that method is that it does not calculate the position of your eyes and because of this, the image will not be as perfect as a 3D model. This can be solved using more advanced techniques that involve tracking eyes, but in that case, the performance will not be in real-time for JavaScript applications.

Optical flow for motion estimation

We saw how to track different objects in a scene and how to make a human interface using them, but we did not see a more generalized approach. When an object changes its position, it moves through a scene and it is interesting to estimate the overall movement of the scene. Here, we will introduce the concept of optical flow, and will see how to use it for object tracking. In the first part, we will focus on the theory and then present two wonderful examples of the optical flow usage. Finally, we will create a simple gesture application.

The Lucas-Kanade optical flow

There are many definitions of optical flow, the main one is: it is the change in structured intensities of an image due to relative motion between the eyeball (camera) and the scene (http://www.scholarpedia.org/article/Optic_flow). According to another definition, it is the distribution of the apparent velocities of objects in an image (http://www.mathworks.com/discovery/optical-flow.html). To get the idea, look at the following image:

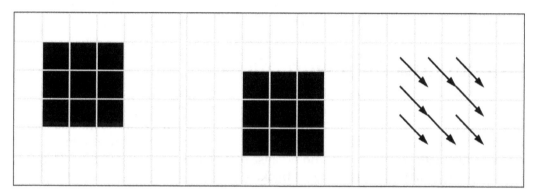

Here, we are just moving a box and the arrows in the third picture show this movement. Simply put, the optical flow shows the displacement of objects. It can be used not only for object tracking, but also for video compression and stabilization. Furthermore, you can get a structure of a scene using the optical flow. For example, if you record a still environment with a moving camera, the objects that are closer to the camera change their destination faster than objects that are far from the camera.

The optical flow can be computed in many ways. The basic assumption of optical flow algorithms is that the object intensities of neighboring frames do not change rapidly. The most popular method is the Lucas-Kanade method. In addition to the previous assumption, it states that the displacement of objects in nearby frames is not large. Moreover, the method takes an NxN patch, typically 3 x 3, around each pixel and it assumes that the motion of all these pixels is the same. Using these assumptions and the knowledge of changes in pixel intensities (gradient) around each pixel of the patch, the algorithm calculates its displacement. The changes in intensities are computed in x and y dimensions and, in time. Here, by time, we mean the difference between the previous and a current frame.

It's only a 3x 3 patch? What should we do with the fast moving objects? This problem can be solved using image pyramids. In this case, we will downsample an image and look for the same movement as that of a 3 x 3 patch, but at a lower resolution.

The other improvement is the iterative Lucas-Kanade method. After getting a flow vector for each pixel, we move pixels by those vectors and try to match the previous and current images. In an ideal situation, those images would be matched, but with real videos there might be errors due to changes in pixels brightness. To avoid an error, we reiterate the process before we get a small error or exceed the maximum number of iterations.

We discussed the theoretical part, now let's move to the two amazing libraries that can provide the implementation of the optical flow. They can be used for different purposes. The core of both libraries is the Lucas-Kanade method.

Optical flow map with oflow

We start with a small library—oflow (`https://github.com/anvaka/oflow`). This is a simple library that just calculates displacement vectors of each patch and returns the overall movement of a scene. We will use this movement to control the ball that we already used in this chapter. Unfortunately, the library does not use an image pyramid to calculate optical flow and because of that, it is better suited for getting the whole scene movement than object tracking.

We start by defining the library in our project:

```
<script src="js/oflow.js"></script>
```

As we did previously, we create a video input and a ball canvas. In addition to this, we add a canvas for displaying the optical flow map with `id='flow'`:

```
<div>
    <video id='videoOut' width='640' height='360' autoplay>
        <source src="/path/to/your/video.mp4">
    </video>
    <canvas id='ballScene' width='320' height='190'></canvas>
</div>
<canvas id='flow' width='640' height='360'></canvas>
```

Next, we define an object that will be used for optical flow calculation. You can create it not only for a video as shown here, but also for a web camera (`WebFlow`) and a canvas (`CanvasFlow`). The `zoneSize` variable defines the half dimension of a patch, which is set to 8 by default:

```
var zoneSize = 8,
        videoElement = document.getElementById('videoOut');
var webCamFlow = new oflow.VideoFlow(videoElement, zoneSize),
```

Here is a short example of what we receive in the end — the video on the left and the directions of optical flow on the right:

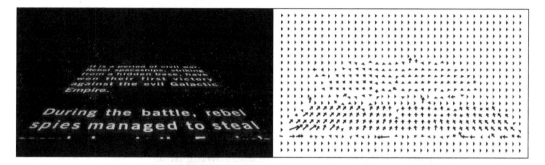

Each arrow shows the movement direction of a patch, of course, there is some noise, but most of the directions show the correct result. How do we receive the result?

After the computation is done for each frame, we need to handle the result. In the following, we receive directions for each patch. Then, we draw arrows that point to the direction of a patch displacement; we multiply that displacement by four so we can see the result in a better manner. You can choose any other multiplier, since it is used only for displaying the optical flow and not for the actual calculation:

```
webCamFlow.onCalculated(function (direciton) {
    flowContext.clearRect(0, 0, sceneWidth, sceneHeight);
    for (var i = 0; i < direciton.zones.length; ++i) {
        var zone = direciton.zones[i];
        drawArrow(flowContext, zone, {x: zone.x + zone.u * 4, y:
zone.y + zone.v * 4}, 2);
    }
```

To calculate the overall displacement, the library just adds together all the vectors. Using the common vector, we draw a ball on its context. If the ball exceeds the screen dimensions, we draw it on the opposite side. The overall direction is returned using the u and v fields of the result:

```
ballContext.clearRect(0, 0, ballSceneW, ballSceneH);
ballContext.beginPath();
ballX -= direciton.u;
ballY += direciton.v;
if (ballX < 0) {
    ballX = ballSceneW;
}
if (ballX > ballSceneW) {
    ballX = 0;
}
```

```
        if (ballY < 0) {
            ballY = ballSceneH;
        }
        if (ballY > ballSceneH) {
            ballY = 0;
        }
        ballContext.arc(ballX, ballY, 10, 0, 2 * Math.PI, false);
        ballContext.fillStyle = 'yellow';
        ballContext.fill();
        ballContext.stroke();
});
```

To start the computational process, just call the following function:

```
webCamFlow.startCapture();
```

After several frames of the video, we get the following result:

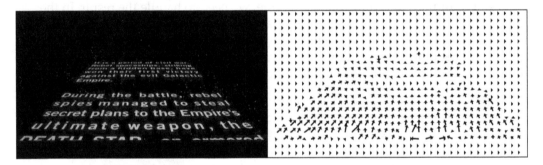

This is where the ball placement is in the first and last frames, respectively:

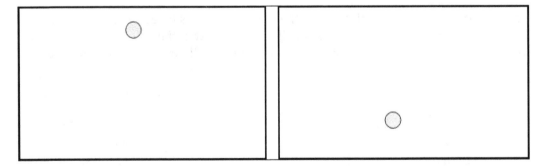

Using this library, it is easy to create a simple game that is controlled by gestures, for example. The library usage is not limited to that and you can create something different very fast.

Track points with JSFeat

The JSFeat library extends the functionality of optical flow and it can even track image points. You can use those points to track objects and control your browser. The implementation of optical flow in JSFeat library uses the iterative Lucas-Kanade method with pyramids and the result it provides is very smooth.

In JSFeat, to work with a video, we need to include an additional JavaScript file, which is provided by this library:

```
<script src="js/compatibility.js"></script>
```

Next, we define a video to be processed and a canvas for displaying the content:

```
<video id="vid" width="640" height="360" autoplay style="display:
none">
    <source src="/path/to/your/video.mp4"/>
</video>
<div>
    <canvas id="canvas" width="640" height="360"></canvas>
</div>
```

There are a lot of variables that need to be defined:

```
var video = document.getElementById('vid');
var canvas = document.getElementById('canvas');
var context, canvasWidth, canvasHeight;
var curr_pyr, prev_pyr, count, status, prev_xy, curr_xy;
```

The last row, from left to right shows: current image pyramid, image pyramid from the previous level, number of points that are tracked, and status of points. The status indicates whether a point has its representation on a new frame; if there is no such point, then the method assumes that the tracking of this point was lost and it is removed from the tracking process. The last two variables contain the point coordinates of the previous and current frames.

We do not provide functions to select original points here, but you can see them in the JSFeat example:
https://github.com/inspirit/jsfeat/blob/gh-pages/sample_oflow_lk.html.

The following function initializes all necessary variables:

```
function init(videoWidth, videoHeight) {
    canvasWidth = canvas.width;
    canvasHeight = canvas.height;
    context = canvas.getContext('2d');
    context.fillStyle = "rgb(0,255,0)";
    curr_pyr = new jsfeat.pyramid_t(3);
    prev_pyr = new jsfeat.pyramid_t(3);
    curr_pyr.allocate(canvasWidth, canvasHeight, jsfeat.U8C1_t);
    prev_pyr.allocate(canvasWidth, canvasHeight, jsfeat.U8C1_t);
    count = 0;
    status = new Uint8Array(100);
    prev_xy = new Float32Array(100 * 2);
    curr_xy = new Float32Array(100 * 2);
}
```

To start getting video frames, we need to call the following function:

```
compatibility.requestAnimationFrame(process);
```

It uses the `process` function to work with each video frame:

```
function process() {
    compatibility.requestAnimationFrame(process);
    if (video.readyState === video.HAVE_ENOUGH_DATA) {
        context.drawImage(video, 0, 0, canvasWidth, canvasHeight);
        var imageData = context.getImageData(0, 0, canvasWidth,
canvasHeight);
```

We copy the points and pyramid variables from the previous frame with the `curr_` prefix to variables with the `prev_` prefix:

```
        var _points = prev_xy;
        prev_xy = curr_xy;
        curr_xy = _points;
        var _pyr = prev_pyr;
        prev_pyr = curr_pyr;
        curr_pyr = _pyr;
```

Next, we compute an image pyramid for the current frame:

```
        jsfeat.imgproc.grayscale(imageData.data, canvasWidth,
canvasHeight, curr_pyr.data[0]);
        curr_pyr.build(curr_pyr.data[0], true);
```

To call a function for optical flow, we introduce four more variables that this function needs. The first variable is `win_size`, which is the size of a patch for searching the flow vector; the `max_iter` variable is the maximum number of iterations; the `eps` variable is the algorithm, which stops updating a point when the movement is less than `eps`; and the `min_eigen_threshold` variable, which is the threshold for removing bad points. The `process` function computes new point coordinates on a new frame. After this, we call the `prune_oflow_points` function. If you continue a video, you can probably loose some points on a future frame. In that case, they will not be tracked anymore and will be removed from the `curr_xy` variable by this function:

```
var win_size = 20;
var max_iter = 30;
var eps = 0.01;
var min_eigen_threshold = 0.001;
jsfeat.optical_flow_lk.track(prev_pyr, curr_pyr, prev_xy,
curr_xy, count, win_size, max_iter, status, eps, min_eigen_threshold);
prune_oflow_points(context);
    }
}
```

Here is the result we received:

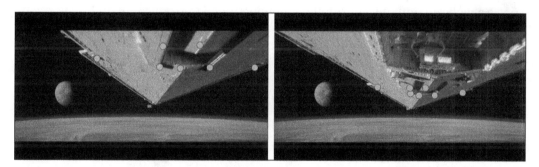

As we can see, all points were successfully tracked; this is an ideal example, where the object was moving smoothly. In many cases, points can be tracked correctly, especially if a video is not edited.

The functionality of the library provides an excellent opportunity to track an object by defining its unique points, for example, you can predefine those points using FAST corner detection from *Chapter 3, Easy Object Detection for Everyone*. In addition to that, you can stabilize a video in real time and do other amazing things with it.

Zooming with gestures

What if we want to extend the functionality a bit? Suppose we want to add a simple zooming feature to our website. We can use the optical flow for that.

To start, we create our content tag we want to zoom with the following style:

```
#content {
    position: absolute;
    margin: auto;
    top: 0;
    right: 0;
    bottom: 0;
    left: 0;
    width: 100px;
    height: 100px;
    line-height: 100px;
    font-size: 10pt;
    text-align: center;
    vertical-align: middle;
}
<div id="content">Content</div>
```

To use a webcam with JSFeat, run the following function from compatibility.js, which simply initializes your camera:

```
compatibility.getUserMedia({video: true}, function (stream) {
    try {
        video.src = compatibility.URL.createObjectURL(stream);
    } catch (error) {
        video.src = stream;
    }
    setTimeout(function () {
        video.play();
    }, 500);
}, function (error) {
});
```

For zooming, we need only two points. So, after receiving the result from the optical flow algorithm, we check whether there are two points and if so, we call the zoom method:

```
jsfeat.optical_flow_lk.track(prev_pyr, curr_pyr, prev_xy, curr_xy,
count, win_size, max_iter, status, eps, min_eigen_threshold);
if (count == 2)
    zoom(prev_xy, curr_xy);
```

The method itself is very simple. We save the original size and change it based on the information we receive from the points of optical flow. We check the distance between two points and if it changed, we change the `<div>` content with respect to it:

```
var size = 100.0;
var content = document.getElementById('content');
function zoom(prev_xy, curr_xy) {
    var prev_d = dist2(prev_xy);
    var curr_d = dist2(curr_xy);
    size = Math.round(size * Math.sqrt(curr_d / prev_d));
    content.style.width = size + 'px';
    content.style.height = size + 'px';
    content.style['line-height'] = size + 'px';
    content.style['font-size'] = (size / 10) + 'pt';
}

function dist2(arr) {
    return Math.pow(arr[0] - arr[2], 2) + Math.pow(arr[1] - arr[3],
2);
}
```

Here is an example of zooming, where we used the Canny edge detector in addition to the whole process:

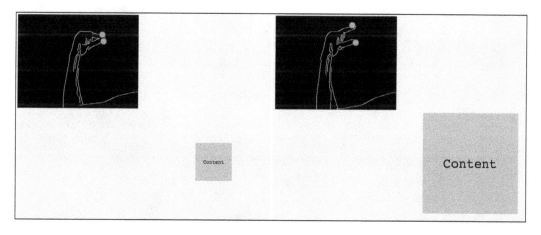

There is no function to find your fingers on a video, so you need to select them before using the zoom function. If you want to find them by yourself, it is all in your hands! Probably, you could create a new era in web browser user experience.

Summary

This is the last chapter of this book. Here, we saw examples that aggregate many techniques from the previous chapters. We covered object detection and tracking by color, which you can use to create your first tracking application very quickly. We explored the power of Head-coupled perspective, which is a new way to present the content on your websites in a fresh manner or create funny browser games with a human interface. In addition to that, the optical flow provides many extensions to this field too. It provides you with an excellent way to track points and objects. Moreover, now you can create a simple application that uses gestures to zoom the web content. The usage of optical flow is not limited to that and is very flexible, and it can be combined with many techniques.

6
What's Next?

You have done a lot so far. Starting from basic math operations to complex filters and object tracking, we reviewed the most popular and most multifunctional libraries on Computer Vision, which are available in the JavaScript world. There are a lot of topics in Computer Vision and image processing, which we did not touch in this book. Here, we will try to provide an idea where you can go next.

First, we will summarize the topics in Computer Vision, which you have already learned. Then, we will discuss why it is so important to use JavaScript in some cases.

Next, we will introduce several JavaScript libraries, which were not covered in the previous chapters. Many of them provide improvements in algorithms and extend applications of Computer Vision in the Web.

We will cover the following topics in this chapter:

- Understanding the importance of client-side scripting
- Overview of some other interesting libraries in Computer Vision

Refresh your memory

In this book, we have applied different image processing and Computer Vision techniques to images and videos. Starting from fundamental math operations, we saw how basic math can be used for different applications and how it is important to know mathematics to understand the basics of image processing. Those operations were extended to provide a clear means of image filtering. The main concept here was the image convolution when a transformation was applied for each image pixel. Then, we followed the path of object detection. We even created our own object detector! The face detection and tracking algorithms showed us that these types of methods can be applied to create a human interface. We saw an example of this in the previous chapter (cube rotation with a head). One of the most exciting methods is optical flow, with the help of which you can easily track objects and create complex programs that are controlled by gestures. Let's have a small exercise. In the following image, you can see that we applied different Computer Vision and image processing methods on an image:

The original image is in color, you can find it in the provided image bundle.

The preceding image is divided into eight parts, and we have applied different algorithms on them. The first part is the original part of an image. The second is the converted into grayscale. Try to guess other ones, we have learnt all of them during the course of the book. If you want to check yourself, look at the answer at the end of this section.

Importance of client-side scripting

So, why do we use JavaScript? We have already addressed this in the preface. Now, you can probably answer it by yourself.

When it comes to practical Computer Vision, many people mention the OpenCV library (http://opencv.org). Yes, it does provide the outstanding functionality for people who do not know much about Computer Vision. Unfortunately, it is written in C++ and does not provide an interface for JavaScript. And if it does, a user needs to install the OpenCV package on their computer, which is not good for the end user, as they would want to use your websites without installing anything.

If you just install the backend library on your side and do the whole computation on your servers, then you will need a ton of clusters to support your website. Even a small portion of Computer Vision algorithms can slow down computer performance significantly. This is probably why you will prefer to use the client-side scripting.

It is now time for JavaScript to show its full potential. Using it, we kill two birds with one stone. Note that:

- There is no need anymore for a user to install anything but a browser (which is usually already installed) on their computer
- JavaScript runs directly on the end user machine, so you do not need to use expensive equipment.

There are already many Computer Vision algorithms implemented in JavaScript. Unfortunately, not as many as in OpenCV, for example. But you can already use the JavaScript libraries and even extend them! We think that you are prepared enough to extend current boundaries of Computer Vision in the JavaScript world.

Here are the answers for the image earlier in this section. The relevant chapter number is written in brackets after each answer. After the grayscale part of the image (1) the answers for image parts from left to right are: histogram equalization (2), blur (Gaussian Blur) (2), Sobel Filter (2), Canny Edge detection (2), feature extraction (FAST features) (3), and finally color object detection (3).

Other interesting libraries in Computer Vision

We already saw a lot of Computer Vision JavaScript libraries, but there are many of them which we did not discuss in the book. Some of those libraries are focused on face and face particle detection, others are a bit more general and implement several object detection techniques.

CCV library and its extensions

Face detection is probably the most popular task in web applications.
One of the original libraries, which provide face detection is the CCV library (`https://github.com/liuliu/ccv`). The main part of the library consists of C functions, but there are JavaScript parts that are responsible for the face detection. There are a lot of libraries which base their face detection on it, for example:

- `http://facedetection.jaysalvat.com`: This is the jQuery library with an easy-to-follow installation guide and API.

- `https://github.com/wesbos/HTML5-Face-Detection`: This library is very easy to use; it detects a face using only the `App.start()` command.

- `https://github.com/neave/face-detection`: This is the modified version of the previous library. It provides functions to work with the `getUserMedia` API.

Face detection and more

There are libraries that tend to provide face detection extensions. Some of them use libraries that are already discussed in this book, for example, the JSFeat library (`http://inspirit.github.io/jsfeat/`).

We start from the Camgaze library (`https://github.com/wallarelvo/camgaze.js`). Its primary focus is eyes detection and gaze prediction.

Another wonderful library is CLMtrackr (`https://github.com/auduno/clmtrackr`). It is an exceptional library for fitting facial models to a face on a video or an image. To understand this better, look at the following image:

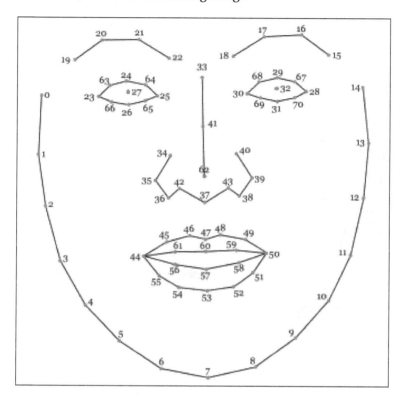

The library tries to fit the facial model point-by-point. With the help of this model, you can precisely track a face or recognize emotions. The author provides a couple of examples where you can perform these tasks. In addition to this, there are examples of face deformation and face masking. For a basic explanation of how this is done, you can follow an excellent overview of that library, which is available at `http://auduno.com/post/61888277175/fitting-faces`.

Object detection with js-objectdetect

We will introduce one more library here. It is js-objectdetect (`https://github.com/mtschirs/js-objectdetect`), which is an excellent library. You may ask, why is that? It provides a lot of trained Haar classifiers, so you can play with them a bit more. In addition to face, eye, and mouth detectors, it contains classifiers for smile, body (full and upper), hands (open and fist), nose, and profile face.

Not all classifiers in the library have the same performance, many of them are sensitive for lighting conditions and noise. But they are totally worth a try!

Summary

We have completed the book. Congratulations! It was an exciting journey for all of us. In this closing chapter, we reviewed methods that we covered in the book, and we saw when it is appropriate to use JavaScript in web projects. Moreover, we prepared you a way for other amazing JavaScript libraries. You can start to build your own projects right now!

Certainly, by now, you have much more experience in the Computer Vision realm. You have built skills to apply very complex Computer Vision and image processing algorithms in your web applications. The Computer Vision world is wide and it always brings something new.

Index

Symbols

<img> tag
  using 38, 39
<video> tag
  using 38, 39

A

advanced image processing
  about 27
  Canny edge detector 27-29
  histogram equalization, using 29-31

B

basic matrix operations 4-7
Binary Robust Independent Elementary Features (BRIEF) descriptors 46
box blur 21, 22
brightness binary features
  using 58-61

C

Camgaze library
  about 92
  URL 92
Camshift
  head tracking 65
Canny edge detector
  using 27-29
Cascade of classifiers 56
CCV library
  about 92
  extensions 92
  URL 92

client-side scripting
  importance 91
CLMtrackr
  about 93
  URL 93
color objects
  detecting 34
  own colors, using 37
  predefined colors, used with tracking.js library 34-36
cube example
  reference link 77
custom tracker
  building 40, 41

D

descriptors
  about 46
  BRIEF descriptors 46
  implementation 47, 48
  matching 47, 48
  object location, obtaining 49, 50
  ORB descriptors 46

E

edge detection
  about 24
  other operators 26, 27
  Sobel filter 25, 26

F

face detection
  brightness binary features, using 58-61
  Haar-like features, using 54-58

displaying 8, 9
image, loading 3, 4
Meanshift algorithm 66
motion estimation
  with optical flow 78

O

objects
  controlling, with head motion 74
  detecting, with js-objectdetect 94
  location, obtaining 49, 50
  simple box, controlling 77, 78
oflow
  URL 80
  used, for calculating optical flow 80-82
OpenCV
  URL 55
optical flow
  calculating, with oflow 80-82
  for motion estimation 78
  image points, tracking 83-85
  Lucas-Kanade optical flow 79, 80
  reference link 79
  zooming feature, adding with
    gestures 86, 87
Oriented FAST and Rotated BRIEF (ORB)
  descriptors 46

P

photos
  people, tagging 63-65
predefined colors
  using, with tracking.js library 34-36

R

Random sample consensus (RANSAC)
  algorithm 49

S

separate convolution 18-21
Sobel filter
  used, for edge detection 25, 26
sort algorithms
  with JSFeat 9-11

T

three.js
  URL 74
tracking.js API
  <img> tag, using 38, 39
  <video> tag, using 38, 39
  about 38
  custom tracker, building 40, 41
  setMaxDimension function 39
  setMinDimension function 39
  setMinGroupSize function 39
  URL 38
tracking.js library
  about 15, 72
  Haar features, using 61-63
  image, loading 16
  installation 16
  JSFeat image formats, converting 16, 17
  object tracking application 72-74
  predefined colors, using 34-36
  URL 15
  used, for tagging 61

Z

zooming
  adding, with gestures 86, 87

Thank you for buying
Computer Vision for the Web

About Packt Publishing

Packt, pronounced 'packed', published its first book, *Mastering phpMyAdmin for Effective MySQL Management*, in April 2004, and subsequently continued to specialize in publishing highly focused books on specific technologies and solutions.

Our books and publications share the experiences of your fellow IT professionals in adapting and customizing today's systems, applications, and frameworks. Our solution-based books give you the knowledge and power to customize the software and technologies you're using to get the job done. Packt books are more specific and less general than the IT books you have seen in the past. Our unique business model allows us to bring you more focused information, giving you more of what you need to know, and less of what you don't.

Packt is a modern yet unique publishing company that focuses on producing quality, cutting-edge books for communities of developers, administrators, and newbies alike. For more information, please visit our website at www.packtpub.com.

About Packt Open Source

In 2010, Packt launched two new brands, Packt Open Source and Packt Enterprise, in order to continue its focus on specialization. This book is part of the Packt Open Source brand, home to books published on software built around open source licenses, and offering information to anybody from advanced developers to budding web designers. The Open Source brand also runs Packt's Open Source Royalty Scheme, by which Packt gives a royalty to each open source project about whose software a book is sold.

Writing for Packt

We welcome all inquiries from people who are interested in authoring. Book proposals should be sent to author@packtpub.com. If your book idea is still at an early stage and you would like to discuss it first before writing a formal book proposal, then please contact us; one of our commissioning editors will get in touch with you.

We're not just looking for published authors; if you have strong technical skills but no writing experience, our experienced editors can help you develop a writing career, or simply get some additional reward for your expertise.

Mastering OpenCV with Practical Computer Vision Projects

ISBN: 978-1-84951-782-9   Paperback: 340 pages

Step-by-step tutorials to solve common real-world computer vision problems for desktop or mobile, from augmented reality and number plate recognition to face recognition and 3D head tracking

1. Allows anyone with basic OpenCV experience to rapidly obtain skills in many Computer Vision topics, for research or commercial use.

2. Each chapter is a separate project covering a Computer Vision problem, written by a professional with proven experience on that topic.

OpenCV Computer Vision Application Programming Cookbook

Second Edition

ISBN: 978-1-78216-148-6   Paperback: 374 pages

Over 50 recipes to help you build computer vision applications in C++ using the OpenCV library

1. Master OpenCV, the open source library of the Computer Vision community.

2. Master fundamental concepts in Computer Vision and image processing.

3. Learn the important classes and functions of OpenCV with complete working examples applied on real images.

Please check **www.PacktPub.com** for information on our titles

Raspberry Pi Computer Vision Programming

ISBN: 978-1-78439-828-6   Paperback: 178 pages

Design and implement your own computer vision applications with the Raspberry Pi

1. Explore the vast opportunities of Computer Vision with the Raspberry Pi and Python.

2. Design and develop webcam and Raspberry Pi based applications.

3. The book features ample screenshots that will offer a play-by-play account on how to implement Computer Vision fundamentals and applications.

OpenCV Computer Vision with Python

ISBN: 978-1-78216-392-3   Paperback: 122 pages

Learn to capture videos, manipulate images, and track objects with Python using the OpenCV Library

1. Set up OpenCV, its Python bindings, and optional Kinect drivers on Windows, Mac or Ubuntu.

2. Create an application that tracks and manipulates faces.

3. Identify face regions using normal color images and depth images.

Please check **www.PacktPub.com** for information on our titles